URGENTLY NEEDED!
Positions Open For
SELF-RESPONSIBLE PEOPLE

Responsibilities Include:
Monitoring and changing unproductive activities, attitudes, emotions, valuing yourself and others; taking control of yourself and creating the good life.

Guaranteed Benefits Include:
Personal power; self-confidence; motivation; self reliance; greater productivity; fuller expression of potential; inner peace; self-esteem; & happiness.

Qualifications:
Only persons who will accept responsibility and accountability for themselves need apply.

Compensation:
Personal fulfillment & professional success.

Equal Opportunity
Apply Within

~ ~ ~ ~ ~ **Comments on "COOKIES"** ~ ~ ~ ~ ~ ~ ~

Bobbi Sims has brought out beautifully a very important principle: how to make conscious choices about your life. That is the only way to achieve inner peace and personal power."

Vijay Jain, M.D. Medical Director Center for Holistic Healing, Cincinnati, OH

"It's the kind of book to keep by your bed or by your easy chair. One of the vignettes will hit a nerve. Somewhere in the volume, Sims has written a homily for your life."

Lela Davis, Beaumont Enterprise

"What an absolutely beautiful book! I began to fold down pages of lines or thoughts I wanted to go back to and now find that more than 3/4 of the book is folded over."

Rosita Perez, CSP, CPAE, National Speaker and Author

"This book speaks to everyone . . . It is also a great source of ideas for talks as well as a quick lift to help one see things from a different viewpoint." *Unity Church of Christianity, Houston, Texas*

Bobbi Sims is anything but powerless. In this book she demonstrates, through delightful and inspiring stories, how to own your power. Every page is a message from the heart. Soothing reading with wisdom and compassion. A bedside table delight.

*Perry A~ Author of **"People are Just Desserts"***

Bobbi Sims shares an inspirational map to the three great gifts of life: personal power, inner peace, healthy self-esteem. Through her life experiences in caring relationships, professional motivation, and facilitation of others' goals, she guides her reader with insight, sensitivity, and with humor. She directs the reader to travel the road to accepting responsibility for control of life's choices. This is a "must read" for those beginning life's journey as well as for those who are seeking positive purpose as they explore life's pathways.

Libby Vernon, Ph.D. Vernon & Associates – Consultants

by
Bobbi Sims

Elàn Publishing
1998

Copyright 1998
By Bobbi Sims
All rights reserved

First Published as:
Making a Difference in Your World.
Copyright 1984 Bobbi Sims
First printing, May 1984
Second printing, October 1985

Library of Congress cataloged in Publication Data
Sims, Bobbi.

1. Meditations. 2. Sims, Bobbi. l. Title. BV4832.2.S527 1983
248.3'4 83-12162 ISBN   0-88289-420-X

Manufactured in the United States of America

First and second editions
Published by Pelican Publishing Company, Inc.
1101 Monroe Street, Gretna, Louisiana 70053

Revised by Bobbi Sims 1998
Don't Let 'em Crumble Your Cookies

Photographs by John Freeman
Drawings by Charlotte Watson & Joy Riddle
Cover Design by David Smith
Title Design by Altek Graphics

Elàn Publishing
PO Box 6956
Corpus Christi, TX   78466-6956

ISBN: 1-879521-12-1

Dedicated to the people who
lived these stories.
Your experiences are serving
as a tremendous teacher for all of us.

Thank you for
turning concepts and theories into realities.

There are two ways of spreading light;
to be the candle or the mirror that reflects it.
Edith Wharton

ACKNOWLEDGMENTS

Thinking about the experiences I might include in this book has created a tremendous amount of gratitude to all the people who have made a difference in my life and the lives of others by sharing their stories. They have contributed to the ongoing growth and understanding of all of us.

I especially want to acknowledge Nina, Ruth, and Helen who gave me great encouragement on the first edition of this book. I am deeply appreciative of Pelican Publishing Company for believing in this book and publishing the first and second editions.

I am especially grateful to my editor Toni Annable for freeing me to let the ideas flow. Her unwavering honesty gave me the ability to fine tune each story.

And special thanks to each of you who have believed in my work, given me support and encouragement. I am deeply grateful.

CONTENTS

THE THREE GIFTS OF PERSONAL RESPONSIBILITY 9

LESSONS FROM NATURE 41

IDENTIFYING FROM THE INSIDE OUT 49

IMPROVING YOUR OPINION OF YOURSELF 57

LIVING IN THE NOW 63

MINDING YOUR ATTITUDES 69

UNDERSTANDING YOUR SELF 85

FEELING YOUR FEELINGS 93

IMPROVING RELATIONSHIPS 105

LESSONS FROM EVERYDAY LIFE 123

ACHIEVING YOUR GOALS 131

LOVE, THE GREAT MOTIVATOR 139

CONNECTING WITH OUR SOURCE 144

EPILOGUE 155

THE THREE GIFTS OF PERSONAL RESPONSIBILITY

PROLOGUE

There is a story about a mother who baked cookies for her children. As she placed a plate on the table she called, "The cookies are ready." As children will, the older ones rushed to the table pushing each other aside, snatching cookies and running off. As the littlest fellow scrambled up to the table and reached for his, there was nothing left on the plate except broken pieces. In a fit of anger, he fell to the floor kicking, and screaming. "Somebody crumbled my cookies!" he wailed.

Many people go about kicking and screaming because their lives are not the way they want them to be. They can't celebrate the goodness that still exists. They focus only on what isn't.

You will recognize these people as the co-worker who is uncooperative, the boss who doesn't credit your abilities, or the family member you are never able to please. You know the ones. Just because these people have had their cookies crumbled, you have a choice as to whether you will give them the power to crumble yours. We can't control how others treat us, however, we *can* control how we let their behaviors affect us. Learning to focus our attention on our internal response to external circumstances is our personal responsibility. This switch in focus allows us to strengthen ourselves and to objectively look at our options.

Like the child out of control, all too often we allow circumstances, situations, or even other people to crumble our cookies and consistently spoil our day and sometimes even our lives. When we do this, we don't realize we are giving over our power of self to external forces rather than taking responsibility for allowing the circumstances to affect us. Each and every one of us have been given the precious gift of twenty-four hours each day. With that gift comes the responsibility of what we make of it and how we live it.

Just as we have a natural law that brings the sun up every morning and down every evening, we have a natural law of the mind. On some level of consciousness, the mind always knows when, where and how we are responsible. As a result, every time we place blame and make an excuse for our situation or circumstance, we create guilt in ourself. That guilt locks us in the prison of our own mind. We are in a prison of our own making, powerless to make change or take action, living the life of a victim. People use blame and excuses to avoid responsibility, to save their self-esteem, to save face or avoid guilt. It may even be learned behavior carried over from childhood. Whatever the reason, it is time to choose a higher, more powerful way to deal with ourselves and our mistakes of omission and commission.

You are either responsible for what happens or the victim of what happens. If you blame others for what happens to you, you have chosen to be the victim and not in control of your life and thus you are powerless. The stories in this book will encourage, motivate, and inspire you to seek the three great gifts self-responsibility bestows:

Personal Power ✦ Inner Peace ✦ and Healthy Self-Esteem

The greatest lesson I have ever learned was a gift from my youngest son, Phillip. It was a few days after the accidental death of David, my oldest son. In our pain, my only surviving child, Phillip and I were attempting to process through the unspeakable thing which had happened. In our grief we talked about his and his brother's childhood. My heart was heavy as we spoke about the difficult times David had gone though when his dad and I divorced. The boys were young at the time. Abruptly, Phillip said to me, "Mother, when you and Dad got a divorce, I made up my mind that this is my life, and I'm not going to let your and Dad's problems spoil it."

I was astonished by his wisdom. You see, he was only ten when he made that decision and now he is thirty. Suddenly, I felt lighter. I was amazed he had accepted responsibility for his own life.

Some people, like Phillip, are born with a sense of self-responsibility. Others have excellent role models who teach them responsibility, like the father of Tiger Woods. In an interview, Mr. Woods said that when Tiger was 7 or 8 years old he asked, "Hey Dad, where are my golf clubs?" His dad responded, "Tiger, whose golf clubs are they? If you want to play golf, you are responsible for knowing where they are and putting them in the car when we are ready to play golf." Mr. Woods was good at teaching his son responsibility. Much later in Tiger's life, he tells of the time Tiger blamed a distraction for a poor shot. Mr. Woods said, "Tiger, distractions are part of the game. You have to learn to play though them." While golfers blame a sudden cough or a puff of wind for a bad game, many others blame external circumstances on how they play the game of life.

Phillip had a big distraction in his young life. Instead of placing blame he learned to accept it as part of living and continued to play the game to win.

All of us are held accountable for our performance in our work. Just as importantly, we need to hold ourselves accountable for how we allow the outside world to affect us. As accountability to ourselves grows, we will receive the precious gifts that responsibility bestows. My hope is that these stories will serve as a guide so you will receive the rewards that accompany personal accountability.

It's YOUR life.

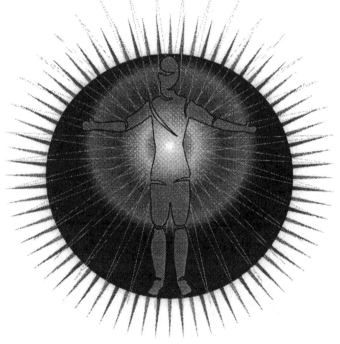

Give <u>Nothing</u> or <u>No One</u> the power to spoil it!

Man is condemned to be free;
because once thrown into the world
he is responsible for everything he does.
Jean-Paul Sartre

Average! Average! I was indignant as I read my evaluation slip. How could this test show I was just average in "personal responsibility." After all, I pay my bills on time, I'm a good citizen, I obey the law, I cause no one harm. I was participating in a spiritual growth group, and I was the only one who was obviously confused about their evaluation. No one in the group received above average. I had no idea what I needed to do to improve and no one could offer me any suggestions. In fact, I don't think any of us had a clue at that time what "self responsibility" was.

That average evaluation haunted me for many years before I began to understand the depths of individual accountability. It wasn't until I began to shift my attention to my internal responses rather than to external circumstances that I began to understand self-responsibility.

I reviewed my life and looked at all the times I had been used, abused, or taken advantage of, and made a discovery. I was the only one who had been consistently present every time I had been victimized. The question I had to ask myself was, "Where was I while all this was happening?"

What a rude awakening. I had shifted my responsibility by focusing on what the other person involved was doing or not doing. I was not innocent! I began the process of understanding that I was either responsible or a victim. By not taking care of myself, I had allowed myself to become a willing victim.

What a discovery!

This objective view of my life and my participation or lack of it, started me on the road to holding myself responsible for my internal life as well as the external response. When you take responsibility for yourself, you stop being a victim.

*Wake up and come to the party,
this is your life.*

As I sat preparing for the day, a still small voice which I have come to know as my inner teacher said, "Wake up and come to the party, this is your life!" Missing the point of waking up to the circumstances in my life, my mind thought it was an idea for a youth program I was putting together. I am embarrassed to say it wasn't until much later that I realized that I had received an injunction from my inner self to take greater responsibility for my life. I was the only one accountable for its course. When I realized my foolishness in thinking it was a message for someone else, I broke out in spontaneous laughter that lasted several minutes.

The party was my life. I needed to wake up to how I was holding someone else responsible for the circumstances at that time. I was the one who was accountable for determining its course. Things don't happen by luck, by waiting, or by blame. It was up to me to define the quality of my life and it's outcome.

Each of us is fully responsible for our choices about all of our life issues. We decide what we want to be about as a human being; We develop our values and ideals. We each get to choose what contribution we want to make to society. We determine the quality of our life.

If you accept this as truth, how different will your life become? We do have all these choices. No one can take away what is a God given gift. We can, however, give over our choice to someone else. We can surrender to circumstances. Yet when we give away our choice, we always feel powerless and victimized.

When we take back responsibility and make conscious choices, we take back our own power. We can enjoy the party and become a full participant in our own life.

*Most folks are about as happy as
they make up their minds to be.*
Abraham Lincoln

All too often I hear the expression, "I'll be happy when..." One young woman said to me, "I'll be happy when I get married." I asked her if she was happy now, and she replied, "No, but I will be when I have a husband." I expressed my conviction that if she wasn't happy as a person, a husband certainly couldn't make her happy. Besides, what a burden being responsible for her happiness would be for him! A husband could add to her happiness or he could detract from it to some degree, but he could not make her what she was not.

I told her that I, too, had nurtured the fantasy that I would be happy when I had the right person to share my life with. Having lived many years without that happening, I finally realized that my problem was that I was not taking responsibility for my own happiness. For a long time I thought it depended upon external conditions and so I was looking for another person to create my happiness for me.

Since external conditions weren't perfect for too long, and since no one showed up to make me happy, I finally made a decision that I would be happy anyway and that I would be willing to be responsible for myself. Immediately my life was transformed.

I have allowed others to add to my happiness, not to be responsible for it. I have even allowed some people to detract from my happiness, though not for very long.

The hardest decision is to be happy in spite of our world not being the way we want it. What does your happiness depend upon?

Feelings don't go away
just because they are tucked away.

Her angelic face, surrounded by golden curls, was now drawn, and her eyes held deep sorrow. It had been over two years since her father died, when Leah, my four year old granddaughter was visiting with me.

My heart grieved for her as I watched her move about without the liveliness she formerly radiated.

Drooping her head she came and sat beside me. In a dejected little voice, she said, "Grandmother, isn't it sad that my daddy had to die?"

"Yes, Sweet Girl, it is." I said. "I miss him too."

As I looked into her desolated little face, I had a flash of insight. It was crystal clear to me that because her father had died, she did not have permission to be happy.

"Leah, if you could make your daddy happy would you do that?" I asked.

"Oh yes, Grandmother."

"Well, let me tell you how to do that. You can make your daddy very happy by being happy yourself. More than anything, your daddy would want you to be happy again."

Instantly, that little girl broke into a big smile, leaped into my lap, and hugged me like I have never been hugged before or ever since. She had been given permission to be happy again. I was filled with joy.

So many people I have known don't have permission to be happy. Because they have done something that caused them guilt or had a great loss, they believe they have to be unhappy forever.

I could give my granddaughter permission to be happy again because she was a child and I was her father's mother. Only you can do that for yourself.

Regardless of mistakes, your history, or the actions of others, it is okay to be happy. Give yourself permission.

Give what you have.
To someone, it may be better than you think.
Henry Wadsworth Longfellow

For years I conducted ten week long personal growth classes. During that time I saw people make changes, become happy and successful, then revert back to their former ways. This was very disheartening to me. I began to study and research what was or wasn't happening. I am sure many things play a part, however, there was one thing that I discovered was consistent. For whatever reason, many people did not have inner permission to achieve their dream. We can spend a lot of time and money figuring out our reason for this sabotage, and occasionally that is necessary. However, in the here and now, we can give ourselves permission to attain what we want and to act in our own behalf.

The following are common permissions people need to move forward with their life. Please add your own. To create results with these permissions, I offer three options. To maximize the effectiveness, use all three.

1. Repeat them before a mirror maintaining eye contact with yourself.

2. Read them into a tape recorder and listen daily until you see the change take place.

3. Stand with one arm stretched out in front of you with the thumb extended. Using your thumb as if it were a pencil, draw the figure eight as though it were laying on its side. As you draw the figure eight, repeat your permissions. This helps integrate the message into both sides of the brain.

Giving Yourself Permission

I give myself permission to:

Be human

Make mistakes

Be wrong

Make poor choices

Have flaws

Be less than perfect

See the reality of my life

Forgive myself

I give myself permission to:

Act in my behalf

Express myself

Have good relationships

Be highly visible

Be heard

Experience all my emotions

Accept my innate talents

Take risks

Prosper and achieve success

Be happy

Enjoy the journey!

Until you love yourself flaws and all,
you will never feel loved by another.

Joanna was a woman heavy with pain as she sat in my office. She said, "For ten years I tried to become what that man said he wanted and I still couldn't please him. No matter what I did, it wasn't enough." She continued, "Before I left I said to him, 'I don't want your expensive gifts, your money, or your social position. All I have ever wanted was for you to love me unconditionally, just as I am.'"

Looking her in the eye I said, "You told the wrong person what you wanted. You needed to say that to yourself." She looked shocked for a minute, then said, "You're right."

Like Joanna, all to many of us look to someone else to love us the way we want or need to be loved, rather than learn to do that for ourselves. The sad thing is, we will not feel loved by another until we extend love to ourselves. Now, let's talk about how to do that.

It took me a long time to understand that unconditional love manifested itself as acceptance. Let's look at a broader view of acceptance. We don't have to like every thing about ourselves to accept even what we perceive as unacceptable. Until we fully accept every aspect of ourselves, both our strengths and shortcomings, we cannot begin to work on our weaknesses. We will not feel accepted by others until we accept ourselves.

Think about what area you have been seeking acceptance in, then see if you are willing to give yourself the acknowledgment you need.

*You will never know how powerful you are
until you exercise your options.*

A dear precious friend was diagnosed with multiple sclerosis a few years ago. It has been hard to watch the body of this high energy business woman deteriorate.

In a discussion with her about her journey, she said, "The turn around came when I was sitting in the bathroom and my muscles were so weak my husband had to lift me from the seat. How humiliating. That was too much!"

She returned to her doctor seeking physical therapy to strengthen her weakening muscles. Patronizingly he said, "Now, you know there is no cure and this is a neurological problem. No use exercising your muscles. If they do not get the signals from the nerves, they will not move." Leaving his office somewhat angry, she began a search for alternative methods of managing her illness. She was determined not to be passive in the progression of her disease.

Along with traditional treatment she studied nutrition, the mind body connection, and started physical therapy. Today she can walk a whole block and take care of her own personal needs. She is even able to continue managing her business.

"Bobbi"she said, " if I had not accepted self-responsibility for my illness, I would not have improved."

We can all learn from her important lesson on taking responsibility for our health. First, we are obligated to give our bodies the rest, exercise and nutrition it needs to preform well. Second, we need to extend love and appreciation to our bodies for serving us so well. All too often we don't appreciate our health until we lose it. We don't appreciate our bodies when they do not meet our ideal. Third, we need to understand that health, illness and healing take place inside our body. When we are ill, doctors can assist the healing process through education, medicines, treatments and sometimes surgery. But ultimately, we heal from the inside.

We must stay attuned to our bodies so we can make the necessary adjustments in our life style to enjoy maximum health.

You cannot keep doing what you have always
done and expect things to get better.

Some time ago, I was on a plane heading back to Corpus Christi from a round of speaking engagements. My seat mate, a young woman in her early twenties, looked miserable. Every line on her face was turned down; her expression was completely forlorn and filled with discomfort. My natural curiosity made me wonder why she was so unhappy.

After we introduced ourselves, I asked, "Are you going to Corpus Christi on vacation, or are you returning home?"

"No, I've just started a job in Corpus Christi but I hate it."

"You've accepted a job that you hate? How sad! What would you rather do?"

"I want to join the Navy."

"It sounds good to me. Why don't you?"

"Well, I don't know how my employers would feel about that."

Surprised, I asked, "Do you need their approval?"

"Well," she said, "I don't know how my parents would feel about it either."

"It's really nice to be considerate." I said. "Tell me how old are you?"

"I'm twenty-two."

"You know," I said, "I have something I'd like to share with you, and it's a gift. My gift is this: you're 22 years old and you don't need anyone's permission to do what you want to do with your life. It's nice to take other people's feelings into account, and you may even want to ask for their opinions, but the ultimate decision is yours. It's your life.

"If you want to use your parents and your employers as an excuse for not doing what you want," I continued, "they're as good a reason as any. If you really want to join the Navy, do it."

The young woman looked at me steadily for a while. Then a smile begin to form as she said, "Well, I guess that's right. Maybe that's what I've been doing -- looking for an excuse."

I said, "Maybe you have. It's no big deal, though, as long as you understand that's what you've been doing -- and as long as you know you have a choice."

After this conversation, I pondered how people allow others to determine their fate. They use them as an excuse for not getting what they want. I thought about all the people I meet, all the complaints I hear, all the excuses people use when their lives aren't the way they want them to be.

I had an idea and I started to put it down on paper. Just before the plane landed, I decided to share my concept with the young woman.

"When we got on this plane I offered you a gift," I said, "and I want you to know you've given me a gift also. This is what I got from our conversation. I think I'm going to use it in my new book." With that, I showed the young woman an advertisement I had written, the one that appears below.

When she read it, the young woman said, "This is great. When your book comes out, I want a copy."

URGENTLY NEEDED!
Positions Open For
SELF-RESPONSIBLE PEOPLE

Responsibilities Include:
Monitoring and changing unproductive activities, attitudes, emotions, valuing yourself and others; taking control of yourself and creating the good life.

Guaranteed Benefits Include:
Personal power; self-confidence; motivation; self reliance; greater productivity; fuller expression of potential; inner peace; self-esteem; & happiness.

Qualifications:
Only persons who will accept responsibility and accountability for themselves need apply.

Compensation:
Personal fulfillment & professional success.

Equal Opportunity
Apply Within

Responsibility is the first step
in responsibility.
William Edward Burghardt Du Bois

Josephine's boisterous behavior was disrupting my class. She exclaimed loudly, "I have a switch that only has two speeds, on and off."

"You created it." I commented. "If it is not serving you well, you might want to re-create it as a variable-speed switch."

Brightening up, she said, "I never thought of that before. I can see my new switch now. It is just like the dimmer switch on my light fixture. I can go at any speed I want."

In that same class Jane remarked that she was a born worrier. I found it very funny to try to imagine a "worry baby," and I quipped, "Since most babies are born either boys or girls, I'll bet you sure attracted a lot of attention." She did not see the humor in this and went on to defend her contention that she was helpless to do anything about her worrying.

Both Josephine and Jane had expressed an attitude that is very common—the belief that the traits and characteristics that people posses have been bestowed upon them by fate. Some people, like Josephine, don't know that they are responsible for creating their approach to life. Others, like Jane, don't want to be responsible.

Believing our experiences are ruled by fate puts us in a position of helplessness. Accepting responsibility for our lives gives us power.

*A man who reforms himself has contributed
his full share towards the reformation of his neighbor.*
Norman Douglas

One of the best investments I ever made was attending a workshop with Dr. Dee Mundschenk. I came away from that seminar with one idea, an idea that gave me back my personal power.

There were thirty-six people in our group, each one a mirror for me. Every time one person complained about what someone else was doing or not doing, Dr. Mundschenk responded with, "What they are doing is not the issue. The issue is, how are you letting their behavior affect you?"

After hearing this said in a number of different ways throughout the day, I finally got it. I finally saw my reflection clearly. I had been using my energy to try to get other people straightened out. Since that didn't work, I was left feeling frustrated and powerless.

I finally realized on a deep level of consciousness that I had no real power to straighten out others. The only real power I have is over me. When I began to spend my energy straightening myself out, my feelings of helplessness were transformed into feelings of personal power.

Where is your focus — on other people's behavior or on your reaction to their behavior?

You give the power you
have over yourself to others
when you make their
behavior the issue.

Trying to control where you
have no control renders you
powerless and thus, the
victim.

The only control you have is
what takes place inside your
skin . . .
> Your thinking
> Your feelings
> Your behaviors
> Your reactions
> Your actions

Remember:
Other People's Behavior
is not the Issue!

The issue is your response!

To maintain your own
power ask yourself:

♦ How am I letting this affect me?

♦ What are my options?

♦ How am I going to respond?

♦ What positive action do I need
to take?

If we loved our neighbors as ourself,
they just might kick us in the shins.

Several friends were having lunch, when the subject of weight gain came up. Virginia shuddered, and with disgust said, "My body is in awful shape." Without thinking, I quipped, "Not really, its in great shape considering that you don't exercise and what you been feeding it." She knows I love her so she wasn't offended. She laughed and said, "A perfect answer."

Afterward, I thought about all the times I had looked in the mirror and was disgusted with what I saw. Unfortunately, all too many of us are not happy with how our bodies look. As evidence of this assumption, I looked at the magazines at the check out in the grocery store. I noted that on the cover of every magazine was an article on weight loss. Discussing this with another friend, she told me about an audio tape she had listened to entitled, "Lighten Up," by Carol Hanson. Her goal is to teach people to love them-selves and to begin with their unacceptable bodies.

While I can't do her message justice, I will share the essence of it as I have applied it. Her instructions were to look in the mirror while still in your in your birthday suit and say to each part of your body, "I love you and appreciate you." As hard as this is for some of us, we only have to do it once before the mirror. After that, on a daily basis, we need to tell each area our body we love and appreciate it. The friend who told me about this concept, tells her body with a bit of humor, " I love and appreciate you for staying around so long and serving me so well." We each have to find our own words, just make sure they are loving and supportive. This takes no extra time if we do this while we are showering or dressing.

With nothing to lose but weight, I was game to experiment with the idea. Slowly but surely, I found it had a profound effect on how differently I ate, exercised and felt, toward myself and others. The logic of this made sense to me. When we dislike another person, they can sense it even when it is not expressed. As a result, they are distant or uncooperative toward us. So when we have disgust toward our bodies, like people, they also become uncooperative with us. We have a war between our physical, mental and spiritual states.

Love and appreciation make a difference in all areas of our life. Are you game to love and appreciate what you dislike most about yourself and observe the outcome?

Head Says

Heart Says

*You are responsible **for** yourself;*
*You are responsible **to** others.*

We cannot discuss personal responsibility without discussing any false sense of responsibility we may be carrying. There are mothers who feel responsible for every choice their child makes. There are spouses who feel responsible for the happiness of their partner. There are people who feel responsible for how other people feel. The list could go on and on.

Many of us have grown up with the teaching, "We are our brother's keeper." When we interpret the teaching to mean we are responsible for another, we can develop a false sense of responsibility. This leads us to believe that we have a power we actually do not. With that false sense of power, we try to control where we have no control. People who feel responsible for others, try to coerce or manipulate them into doing what they think is right. They feel compelled to do this or they have failed in their duty.

Feeling responsibility *for* can lead us to help people who haven't indicated they want help. When we do this, we rob them of their dignity and send the message that they are not capable of taking care of themselves. We also help people who won't be responsible for themselves, which results in keeping them powerless.

We can be responsible *to* people who are ill, who are out of work, who are in financial despair, or who are unable to help themselves. Former President Carter took on a responsibility to help others in need through his outstanding work with Habitat for Humanity. He is a positive role model for demonstrating our responsibility to humankind. We can think of many who have helped in their own way. People like Jerry Lewis and his Telethon, Mother Theresa, Martin Luther King, Bob Hope, perhaps your next door neighbor, or you yourself. These are people who cared about others without regard to personal gain. They only had a need to serve.

We can influence others through our character, by the quality of our own lives, and the service we provide. We can encourage people to believe in their own abilities, and offer support as they develop their life skills. I would not be where I am today, without the people who believed in me and my work when my own belief was faltering. These are really great gifts to give people.

We are responsible for treating people with dignity, respect and with

-30-

fairness. In business, we are responsible for providing the kind of service we promise to deliver. We are not responsible for what the customer does with the end product.

In relationships, we are certainly responsible to support the well being of the other, by being who we are. We are *not* responsible for their feelings, failures, or how they allow life to affect them.

Before taking on the responsibility for another, ask yourself, "Have they asked me for help or advice? Will the recipient welcome my good intentions to help them? Or am I just being presumptuous enough to think that I know what is best for the other person?"

Self-Responsibility Bestows Three Great Gifts

Our deepest fear is not that we are inadequate.
Our deepest fear is that
we are powerful beyond measure.
Nelson Mandela

Even babies start off in the world using their power to get their needs met. Those tiny little beings are able to learn to sit, crawl, walk and talk on their own. We delight in their ability, until they cross the line of how we want them to be. Then adult power is used to direct, abuse, crush, or manipulate them.

If this occurs, a child begins to *feel* powerless, or fears the power of others. He or she views power through the eyes of powerlessness or abuse. This leads to a life of being a victim; a mindset that good things happen because of "luck." Power for children like this is externally controlled. As long as they are focused on those who control and manipulate, it's difficult to find their own power source from within.

Shirley called me up and said, "I don't know if I should leave for my trip to see my mother tonight or wait until in the morning. I don't know what I should do." Shirley was looking for her answer from an outside source. My response was, "There isn't a right or wrong time to leave. Figure out what you want to do and do it." So it is with life! We must decide what we want and do it!

As we have already learned in our first story, a child is fortunate indeed to have a parent like Mr. Woods who nurtures and teaches how to be responsible for the use of personal power. As adults, we can then exercise our responsibility to create our own life rather than a life imposed by others. This fortunate person, though listening to others, is led from within when making their choices. They claim their own power and do not depend on "luck" for success.

Power translates as energy or ability to act. It is inherent in everyone. Like electricity, power lies dormant until we use it. It can be used for good or evil.

Personal power is acting upon your options..
You will never know how powerful you are
until you exercise your options.
Unknown

An ordinary woman named Paula Rosenstein had a strong desire to help prevent child abuse. She had a vision of trained volunteers who could make a significant impact for families. She researched the idea and reported her findings to the Department of Welfare in Plano, Texas where she found a department head receptive to her concept. That was 25 years ago. Today, Family Outreach, a family support center of volunteers, operates centers across Texas. Through this joint venture, parents can get individual counseling, have home visits, attend support groups or participate in educational programs. Paula viewed power through the eyes of love and compassion resulting in impacting the lives of thousands. Contrast this with the inappropriate use of power.

Remember the young cadet who killed a one time friend on the order of his jealous lover? He violated both legal and moral laws to win the love of an unworthy person. His use of power brought devastation to many people and stunned the nation.

How we view power determines whether we fear it or embrace it. I suspect we don't fear power itself, we fear the responsibility that goes with it. We are empowered in many ways. Gaining knowledge, learning skills, and accepting positions of supervision are some of the paths to empowerment. Some of us even go to the Master Creator for empowerment.

Regardless of how we acquire it, we experience the positive aspects of power when we accept responsibility for how we use it. Whatever our history, the more self-responsibility we accept, the greater the reward of power. It's a gift.

I want the understanding which bringeth inner peace.
Helen Keller

Inner peace is a state of well being that is sought by everyone. The paths to inner peace are many and varied. We can get there within minutes through meditation. However, it doesn't keep us there. To live peaceably we must live in a state of accountability to ourselves, living responsibly in accordance with our personal values, our spiritual values, and our work ethics.

First and foremost, we must begin by making peace with our self. Some of us are so idealistic, we can never meet our standards and expectations. We don't allow for our human imperfections. We can view our self with a compassionate heart only when we fully realize we are *becomers* not *arrivers*. We are a work in process; growing, learning, relearning, failing, succeeding and always changing.

The ability to respond is encapsulated in the word responsibility. We often see ourselves with disapproval as though the ability to respond differently did not exist. Consider that all of us are doing the best we can with the abilities we have. We are always responsible for our responses, but not guilty. Yes, responsible, not guilty.

Guilt comes either from denying responsibility or from our self-condemnation. What we need is forgiveness, not judgment. Judgment does not make us better people. What we do not forgive disturbs our inner peace. When we forgive another, it does not mean we sanction their behavior. Granted, a perpetrator may not deserve forgiveness. However, you deserve the peace that comes from letting it go. Forgiveness, simply stated, means to let go. It's history. It's over. Move on.

Understanding helps us develop compassion for ourself and others. We will not find peace until we find forgiveness.

Jess, a business man of 55, said, "I will never forgive my parents for what they did to me."

I never knew what they did that was so unforgivable. What is interesting is that the unforgiven people were occupying space in his mind and emotions and he was the one paying the rent on their occupancy. Jess wasted a lot of his energy hating them when he could have used it to make a better contribution to society and lead a fulfilling life.

Ginny said, "I cannot forgive myself for not attending college." She could have used that same energy to continue her education instead of staying angry with herself. Forgiveness is not easy. It is essential if we wish to have inner peace.

When we step back and view our behaviors and reactions as what we did rather than who we are, it is easier to forgive. After all, mistakes are like flats. Just fix them. If they aren't fixable, forgive them and move ahead. Life is too precious to do otherwise.

We can maintain inner peace when we live in harmony with our ethical, moral and spiritual values.

The question is,
are you working to look good or become good?

Sitting in an audience with professionals from around the country, I wondered why I was giving up a weekend and spending a few hundred dollars to hear Dr. Scott Peck speak. As he began to talk about the detrimental aspects of those *pursuing* self-esteem rather than developing character, I knew why I was there. He was confirming what I had observed in the hundreds of people with whom I had worked. Self-esteem is a result of the quality of the lives we are living, not a goal we pursue. It's a by-product -- not a destination.

How often do you look at someone and think, "Wow, they look confident and assured. I wish I could be like that?" After speaking at a large convention, a successful attorney came up to me and said, "Bobbi, I have three post graduate degrees and I still don't feel like I am enough." Those who envied his status would have been as surprised by his confession as I was. His low self-esteem was not visible to anyone around him.

I have observed defensiveness, blame, and denial in the workplace for years as well as in people's private lives. These are learned behaviors for protecting our self image. In reality, it doesn't fool anyone including the person who is doing it. Bluntly, it doesn't work.

A couple from one of my retreats was in my office. On the surface they appeared to have all the ingredients to be happy and successful. As each attempted to explain their point of view, the other jumped in defensively. Neither was able to understand the others' point of view. They were both so busy protecting their meager self-esteem that they had no ears for understanding and resolving their conflict.

What we need to pursue is personal responsibility which requires the willingness to do what is right, even when no one is looking. We must learn to admit when we have been wrong or made an error, and to apologize or make amends when we need to do so. After all, we go to bed and get up with ourselves every day for our whole lives. It is our view of our *self* that is important, not the view of others. Our view needs to be based on respect for our actions and inactions. Self-responsibility is the foundation for self-esteem. The more accountable we become to ourselves, the healthier our self esteem becomes. When we are willing to become personally responsible, we give ourselves the gift of self-esteem as a reward.

Acceptance without action is complacency.
Acceptance plus action is empowerment.

Taking car trips alone are times that I have come to treasure. It's great contemplation time. On such a trip, I asked God, "If I could ask for the greatest gift in the whole world, what would it be." The still voice that I have come to as my inner teacher answered, "Acceptance."

"Acceptance!" I exclaimed. In my disappointment, I thought I must not be hearing right. Then I heard, "Think about it!"

For the next two hours I pondered the deeper meaning of acceptance. Realizing the source of all unhappiness was lack of acceptance, I could see the gift. Also, I became aware of a major problem in human relationships, be it personal or professional. That problem is lack of acceptance of each other. Then I made my greatest discovery. "Acceptance is unconditional love in action."

When asked, audiences all across the country tell me they have trouble accepting anything they can't sanction, approve of, or agree with. I am suggesting we don't have to like it, agree with it, or approve of anything to accept something as fact. What is, is! What isn't is not! Not accepting what is, or isn't does not change the fact and makes our life miserable. What we can't accept, keeps us frozen in powerlessness. Until we get to acceptance, we are not decompressed enough to see what our options are to make the most of the situation or what actions we need to take to improve or change.

Are you frozen in time from lack of acceptance? Think about it. It's easy to thaw out!

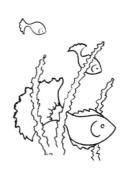

It's Your Life. . .
You are responsible for its quality!

You are responsible *for* you....
You are responsible *to* others.

You are responsible for how you let life affect you.
What is, is! What is not, is not!
You are responsible for your response
to what is and what is not.

You are responsible for :
Your thinking , your actions, your choices, your attitudes,
What you put into your body,
What you say,
Your reactions, your feelings,
Your determination,
Your half of each of your relationships,
Your goals and accomplishments,
Your luck and your happiness.

You are power-FULL
When you accept responsibility.
You can use that power to get your wants and needs met
In such a way that allows others to meet their needs also.

You are not alone.
You are empowered by the Master Creator.
With Him as your partner,
You create your world together.

Acceptance without action is complacency.
Acceptance plus action is empowerment.

Taking car trips alone are times that I have come to treasure. It's great contemplation time. On such a trip, I asked God, "If I could ask for the greatest gift in the whole world, what would it be." The still voice that I have come to as my inner teacher answered, "Acceptance."

"Acceptance!" I exclaimed. In my disappointment, I thought I must not be hearing right. Then I heard, "Think about it!"

For the next two hours I pondered the deeper meaning of acceptance. Realizing the source of all unhappiness was lack of acceptance, I could see the gift. Also, I became aware of a major problem in human relationships, be it personal or professional. That problem is lack of acceptance of each other. Then I made my greatest discovery. "Acceptance is unconditional love in action."

When asked, audiences all across the country tell me they have trouble accepting anything they can't sanction, approve of, or agree with. I am suggesting we don't have to like it, agree with it, or approve of anything to accept something as fact. What is, is! What isn't is not! Not accepting what is, or isn't does not change the fact and makes our life miserable. What we can't accept, keeps us frozen in powerlessness. Until we get to acceptance, we are not decompressed enough to see what our options are to make the most of the situation or what actions we need to take to improve or change.

Are you frozen in time from lack of acceptance? Think about it. It's easy to thaw out!

LESSONS FROM NATURE

*Nature and books belong
to the eyes that see them.*
Ralph Waldo Emerson

Yes, God gave us a rose garden and
we are unhappy because it is full of thorns.

For much of my life I have had an attitude of "Yes, but": "Yes, it would be exciting to be a writer, but I am an ordinary person"; "Yes, but it shouldn't be that way"; "Yes, you are right, but. . . "

I heard myself negating the "yeses" in my life with the "buts." I was spending so much energy complaining about the "buts" that I was not acknowledging and enjoying the "yeses.

Now every time I hear myself say, "Yes, but," I am aware that I am resisting acceptance of what is.

All beliefs that I may have about what should be will not make any difference to what is. Changing the "but" to "and" allows me to accept what is. That acceptance brings me peace of mind and happiness.

Yes, I am an ordinary person, and I am doing extraordinary things with my life. Yes, you are right, and it pains me to agree with you. Yes, it shouldn't be that way, and that is the way it is.

I see life as a rose garden. It has its beauty, its color, its fragrance and it is also full of thorns. Accepting the thorns as part of the garden has released me to enjoy the flowers.

Yes, life is beautiful, and it has its thorns.

> *By virtue of being born to humanity,*
> *every human being has a right to the*
> *development and fulfillment of his*
> *potentialities as a human being.*
> Ashley Montagu

As I contemplated the potential in us all, I remembered the giant pecan trees along the creek banks in Central Texas where I grew up. I recalled how they sprouted and grew without any help from anyone.

Those magnificent trees have always fascinated me. They fascinate me even more when I stop to think how each one started out as a small pecan. One little nut has the potential to become a giant tree that provides us with shade and food. I don't understand the mystery of how that happens, yet I have lived long enough and seen it happen often enough to know that it is so.

If the pecan is to become a giant tree it cannot be eaten. Instead it becomes a seed. This seed has to come out of its shell in order to grow into a tree. As it grows toward maturity, the tree must face droughts, storms, and other natural perils. Each time the tree survives adversity it gains in strength and stature. It takes many years for the tree to reach its full maturity and bear pecans.

So it is with us. We too have to come out of our shells and risk adversity to grow toward our potential. We humans have at least as much potential as a nut! We don't have to understand this potential to use it. We just need to acknowledge it.

Are you acknowledging and using your potential?

But what is happiness except the simple
harmony between a man and the life he leads
Albert Camus

The Frio River in South Central Texas is a magnificent, beautiful, crystal-clear river. Riding its rapids on an inner tube is one of my favorite forms of recreation.

The first time I rode the rapids I experienced both fear and delight. The fear was almost as strong as the delight. As I went through those powerful rapids I had no control—I went where they took me. The fear and tension came from wanting to be in control. As I began to let go, stopped trying to stay in control, and learned a few ways that I could protect myself, there was less fear and more delight. Once I turned loose of my need to control the situation, the Frio could provide me with both recreation and relaxation.

After becoming aware of my need to control the river I began to observe how often I wanted to stay in control of my life. Every time the need to control was present, so was fear and tension. Just as I can't control the river, I really don't have the power to control many of the situations I encounter or the actions of other people. When I shift my attention from controlling to guiding myself through situations and relationships, the tension and fear disappear.

When we don't attempt to control it, life becomes more pleasurable. Are you attempting to control your life, or moving in harmony with it?

Adversity introduces a person to himself
Epictetus

A good tonic for clarifying the mind and soul is working in flower beds. Once, as I laboriously worked to get out the roots of the Bermuda grass that had invaded my flower beds, I became aware of how hard I was striving to get out every tiny little root. Then I remembered my Granddad, who was probably the greatest influence in my life, and how he would come by where we were working on the farm and say, "Get all those roots or the weeds will be right back." I smiled to myself as I thought of that lesson, and felt satisfied as I continued digging to "get all those roots." I began to reflect upon the lesson to see if it applied to the problems of life as well as to weeds.

In my dealings with people, all too often I observe them hard at work attempting to cure the symptoms of their problems rather than getting at the root causes. Reflecting on my own life, I realized that problems or unhappy situations keep reappearing when I only deal with them on the surface.

Go for the roots of the weeds. Get to the bottom of difficulties in troubled relationships, communication breakdowns, and life's other problem.

You are the bows from which
your children as living arrows are set forth.
Kahlil Gibran

While I was conducting a class for a group of teen-agers, three of them asked me to talk with their mothers about their overprotectiveness. I could understand the teens point of view, and thought about how I could get it across to their mothers.

Standing before the mothers, I announced that some of their children had asked me to deliver a message. I decided to do this by telling a story.

"The story is about a beginning gardener. This gardener found rich, fertile soil under a large oak tree. He had it tested and cultivated. It was perfect soil. When he purchased some plants from a nursery, he got very specific instructions on how to plant them. He was very careful to follow these instructions and to water the plants regularly.

"Time passed. Still the garden didn't grow. The gardener went back to the nursery to find out what was wrong.

"The nurseryman asked him a number of questions, but was unable to determine the problem. Finally, he asked where the garden was located. The gardener replied, "Under the protective shade of a big oak tree.""

""That is your problem," the nurseryman explained. "Gardens don't grow in the shade of trees.""

Mothers, your children will not grow well in your shadows.

-46-

*There is only one corner of the universe
you can be certain of improving,
and that's your own self.*
Aldous Huxley

Tomatoes were selling for ninety-eight cents a pound in the grocery store. Growing in my backyard were tomatoes on the verge of ripening. There is nothing quite like growing your own, especially when they are so expensive in the store.

I did everything I could think of to hasten the growing process. The plants didn't ripen any faster. As I began to study my tomatoes I realized that ripening and maturing were the same process: when the tomato ripened it was mature. I could be helpful by supplying water and fertilizer, the tomato had to mature by itself.

It occurred to me that people were the same way. Each person has to do his own maturing. We can give each other support, yet each of us is responsible for his own growth. As a parent, and human-growth educator it was a relief to me to realize where my responsibility ended.

As I continued to study my garden I noticed that some of the tomatoes were like tiny hard green knots—they did not look as good as the ones on the verge of ripeness. When I looked at the more desirable tomato, I realized that it, too, had once been a tiny, hard, green knot. It had gone through different stages of growth, and each stage had been necessary. People, too, are in different stages of growth. Some stages are more appealing than others, yet all stages are necessary steps to maturity. Each stage can be seen as part of the maturing process.

As I worked the bed where the tomatoes were growing, I saw the other fruits and vegetables I had planted. Each was very different from the others; the tomato was not like anything else growing in the bed. I realized that it is also a fact that I cannot be like anyone else. My son can only be himself, not the way I want him to be. There is as great a variety in people as there is in fruits, vegetables, and flowers. As delicious as I find tomatoes, many people don't like them. So it is with people. Not everyone is going to like me—or you—as wonderful as we may be.

I turned back to the tomatoes wondering what else they had to say to me. As I studied them this time, I became conscious of the fact that each tomato was dependent for its growth on the vine itself, and on the soil, the sun, and the rain. I remembered my own struggle to be independent, how I went through a stage of thinking I did not need anyone. How wrong I was! There are many things I am unable to do for myself—like take out my own appendix, build my own house, or repair my own car. Each person has a talent and we are all dependent on one another as well as the Source of who we are.

It also occurred to me that the tomato would mature as long as it was attached to the vine. It had no power to prevent its own growth. Only in the human form do we differ; as people, we can prevent our maturing. We don't mature when we are stuck in an old pattern of thinking and behaving. We can grow toward maturity only when we are willing to open our mind and look for constructive ways to think and behave. I have not only enjoyed raising and eating tomatoes, I have also enjoyed what they have taught me about myself and other people.

IDENTIFYING FROM THE INSIDE OUT

*A sense of identity is so vital that a person
ultimately must find some means of satisfying it.*
Erich Fromm

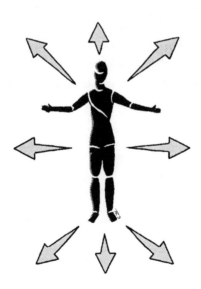

God is thy father, man is thy brother.
Lamartine

When I was a child, people often told me I looked like my mother, and that comparison made me furious. As we both have gotten considerably older and I see how well my mother has held up, that comparison gives me hope.

For the last few years I've been looking at the physical characteristics and genetic strengths and weaknesses that I have inherited from my parents. I have also become conscious of attitudes and behavior patterns that I learned from them. Yes, I have inherited much from my parents, and I am not limited to that inheritance or that identity.

As I began to extend my identity beyond that of my parents, I started to see both them and myself as God's children, as equals. When I focus on that, the limits of who I am were immediately expanded.

If we have inherited genetic characteristics from our earthly parents, I thought, maybe we have some kind of similar inheritance from the Creator of this universe. I don't think God is freckled and redheaded, as I am, so what might I have inherited from him?

As I contemplate His nature, I see Him as love and energy—as creative, as knowing, as emotional, as purposeful. Could His nature also be our nature? Choosing to believe that we are created in His image and have inherited His nature has motivated me to change my identity to "God's child" and to work to accept my inheritance.

Who are you identifying with, and how is it affecting you?

I am not only the actor,
but the director of the acting.
Roberto Assagioli

One of the most frequent goals my students speak of is gaining a sense of identity. Being told who we are is not meaningful, identity can only be experienced, and it is only from the experience that real meaning is derived.

Psychologist J. F. T. Bugental defines a sense of identity as "the sense of 'being there' in one's life." This sense is the opposite of feeling like a passive spectator, of lacking direction.

Society conditions us to do and to have. It does not condition us to be. Our identity comes from our being. If we are identifying with what we do, and something prevents us from continuing to do it, then our identity is gone. If we have been identifying ourselves through what we have and we lose what we have, we lose our identity at the same time that we lose our possessions.

Identity is from the inside out, not the outside in. Experience is what reminds us that we have power to make choices, expand our horizons and move forward.

Remember always that you have not only the
right to be an individual;
you have an obligation to be one. You cannot make any
useful contribution in life unless you do this.
Eleanor Roosevelt

Ask children who they are and they point to their bodies. It seems our bodies provide our first sense of identity. Some of us get stuck in that identity longer than others.

For more years than I care to admit my identity was my freckles and red hair. I thought that freckles and red hair were the worst things that could happen to anyone. No one told me I was cute, let alone pretty. I was always "Freckles" or "Carrottop." When I looked in the mirror, that was who I saw. No one told me I was more than my physical appearance, and I did not have enough sense to figure it out for myself.

A most gorgeous woman was in one of my classes. She had flawless skin and long, dark, thick lashes. Since I have freckled skin, and invisible lashes those were qualities I really admired. As I expressed this admiration to her one day, she said, "Yes, but look, I have this mole right here." My hunch is, that every time she looks in a mirror she sees her mole, not her beauty.

After trying every cream on the market, I still have my freckles. I also know now that I am a lot more than my skin. When I thought of myself as "freckles and red hair," I was unhappy and unsuccessful. That identity robbed me. When I realized that I am more than my physical appearance, I got my power back.

Yes, you have a physical state of being, and you are more than that.

*I am the only person that fools
me into believing I am less of a
person than I am.*
James Walt

For the first thirty years of my life I was unconscious, although I did not know it at the time. Looking back, I see it was as though I was in a deep sleep. As I began to awaken, I began to experience life.

Up until that time I had merely functioned. In fact I functioned rather adequately in some ways. As a housekeeper, for example, I knew the best brand of wax to buy and I had every towel folded perfectly in the closet. I functioned adequately as a seamstress, cook, and gardener. Those are predictable roles in which one can function fairly well while unconscious.

All I could bring to my early roles as a wife and mother were my preconceived notions of what a good wife and mother was supposed to be. These preconceptions precluded experiencing these roles in a meaningful way. Since my ideas were rather narrow they didn't allow for much spontaneity or joy.

When I started to become conscious of being more than my roles and their functions, I began to experience a true sense of self. I realized that I existed before I was a wife and mother, therefore, those roles were not all I was. Being more than my roles enabled me to experience more freedom and creativity to be more effective in them.

Those roles are completed now and I still exist. I am especially glad that I learned I was more than a mother before my boys left the nest so that my identity was not shaken once they were gone.

Many people are drawn to my classes when their roles or functions change. They come in feeling lost. When they become conscious of being more than what they do, they get back their power to create a full life.

*What lies behind us and what lies before us
are small matters compared to what lies within us.*
Ralph Waldo Emerson

In class one night a woman announced that she was a "foodaholic." I asked her if that was who she was, or if that was the way she behaved. She looked puzzled and said, "Is there a difference?" She hadn't separated who she was from what she was doing.

When conducting in-service workshops for teachers, I ask them if they see their students as their behavior. Usually about 75 percent of them say they do.

I explain that if a student is his behavior, then he has no power to be different. For instance, I continue, we all have a need for recognition. If a student does not receive recognition for positive behavior, he may develop negative behavior to get the recognition. Either way the behavior is learned and can be unlearned.

"The student, you, and I are all responsible for our behavior," I conclude. "Since we existed before we behaved the way we do, that is not who we are. Being more than our behavior, we can control it rather than let it control us."

When I see myself or others as our behavior, I limit us all. When I see us as being more than that, I see the power to change that behavior.

Yes, you are responsible for your behavior, and you are more than your behavior.

A life spent in making mistakes is not only more honorable
but more useful than a life spent in doing nothing.
George Bernard Shaw

Show me a person who has failed at something and we will be looking at a person who has achieved something. Success and failure are as linked as roses and thorns. Failure demonstrates that an attempt has been made. People who are attempting things at least win admiration for their efforts.

Yet I encounter many people who are frozen with fear of failure. They have an unrealistic picture of themselves, of others, and of life itself. Remember, Thomas Edison and Babe Ruth failed more times than they succeeded, yet we honor them for their successes. Looking at successful men and women and seeing how many times they failed before they found success might help us transform our assessments of ourselves.

For the first thirty years of my life I played it safe, didn't fail at much, and didn't succeed at much. Since then I've become experimental and attempt a lot. I sometimes fail and I often succeed.

When I fail at something, I acknowledge the failure and then tell myself I am more than the failure. It is awareness of being more than the failure that empowers me to keep on keeping on.

Ever feel like a failure? Remind yourself that while you are responsible for your failures, you are more than those failures.

I AM

I have a mind, body, emotion, and spirit,
 Yet, I am more than this
I am more than my physical appearance
 I am more than my social position
I am more than my profession
 I am more than my behavior
I am more than my gender
 I am more than my financial status
I am more than my history
 I am more than my education
I am more than my failures

I am the performer -- not the performance
I am the thinker -- not the thought
 I am the feeler -- not the feeling

I can let my performance affect me
 or I can affect my performance
I can let my actions affect me
 or I can affect my actions
I can let my feelings affect me
 or I can affect my feelings
I can let my circumstance affect me
 or I can affect my circumstance

I am a person of change
 I am a person of choice
I am a person of growth
 I am a person of worth and value
I am a center of consciousness
 I am one of God's wondrous creation
 I AM

IMPROVING YOUR OPINION OF YOURSELF

*As soon as you trust yourself,
you will know how to live.*
Goethe

The third characteristic of a high achiever
is he is not immobilized by perfectionism.
Charles Garfield

Julie had not been doing very well in school. Her mother told me that she had discovered that Julie was writing her papers and not turning them in. The reason she was not turning in her papers was that she had not finished them. Her mother added that her daughter was a perfectionist and that everything had to be just right or she wouldn't have any part of it.

"Suppose you came to my house and told me you were hungry and that your favorite sandwich was ham and cheese on rye," I said to Julie. "Then when I went to fix the sandwich I found I had only ham, cheese, and whole-wheat bread. Would you then refuse to eat?"

"No," she responded. But it was clear that was exactly what she was doing in school.

One of the biggest surprises I ever had in conducting classes was working with a group of CETA participants. These were people who had not been able to get or hold jobs. I discovered that the majority of them were perfectionists who had let their perfectionism immobilize them. Like Julie, if they couldn't do well, they wouldn't do anything at all.

Some people use their perfectionism to drive themselves to the top, while others are paralyzed by it. In either case they are victims of low self-esteem. They are always focusing on what they don't do rather than on their accomplishments.

Before leaving class one evening a very successful woman related some of her shortcomings to me. Looking directly into her eyes I said, "You really aren't good enough for yourself, are you?" Her eyes welled up with tears and she murmured, "That's what I've been saying to myself, isn't it?"

Are you good enough for you?

Enlightenment is the absence of comparison.
Paul Brenner, M.D.

Jean was a tall, willowy brunette with flawless skin. She sat before me looking miserable, and told me that other women made her feel inferior.

"How do other women make you feel inferior?" I asked.

"Well, my chin recedes a bit, and my breasts are flat. My hair is too curly . . . " and she recited a long list of "flaws."

"Jean, do you always compare yourself to other women?"

"Yes, I do, and there is always someone prettier."

"When you find someone with features you would like to have, does that mean you are not okay as you are?"

"Of course."

Like Jean, many of us make ourselves feel inferior or inadequate by comparing ourselves to others. If we've been feeling pretty good about ourselves, this is a sure way to bring ourselves down. There will always be someone around more talented, more intelligent, better educated, better looking, wealthier, more successful than we are.

I explained to Jean that for a long time I, too, had made myself miserable by making comparisons. However, I'd decided I had suffered long enough. Now I look at people as flowers, each one unique. Roses can't be like buttercups, or daisies like thistles. Each has its own beauty and its own niche to fill.

The choice is yours, you can continue feeling inferior by comparing yourself to others, or you can accept and enjoy your own uniqueness. Just know that you are creating your own feelings either way.

What makes men good is held by some to be nature,
by others habit or training, by others instruction.
As for goodness that comes by nature, this is plainly not within our control,
but is bestowed by some divine agency on certain people who truly deserve
to be called fortunate.
Aristotle

Occasionally I find a person who wants to participate in one of my classes and cannot do so for financial reasons. Sometimes I am willing to invest in people and encourage them to participate, with the agreement that they will pay when they can.

I made this offer to one woman who became far more successful in her business after participating in the classes and began to achieve recognition in her community.

This woman never paid me and I suppose her guilt bothered her. Every time we met she said, "I feel so bad because I have not paid you anything." Over a two-year period this statement was repeated to me several times. Finally I inquired very softly, "Do you want to know why you feel bad?"

"Yes, why?" She responded.

I said to her, "You gave your word and you haven't kept it."

She is a mirror for me. Every time I give my word and don't keep it, I feel bad. This does not have to be over something major, like a financial obligation. It can be as simple as saying, "I'll drop you a line" and not doing it. When I become conscious that I've given my word and not kept it, I correct the situation as soon as possible. Then I can feel good about myself again.

How do you feel when you've given your word and not kept it?

If you accept your own limitations
you go beyond them.
Brendan Francis

As a human-growth educator, I sometimes feel that I am one of the most fortunate people in the world. My students teach me far more than I teach them because they share their thoughts, conflicts, and frustrations with me. As they do, I often begin to see patterns emerging. A pattern that I see consistently is one where people focus on getting their needs met by others, rather than focusing on how they can meet their own needs.

As people confide in me what they want in relationships —whether it's acceptance, respect, love, or forgiveness—I usually find that these same people are unwilling to give to themselves what they are expecting from someone else.

I know that in my own personal life, when I quit rejecting some part of me and accept myself as I am at the moment, I am no longer overly concerned about whether someone else accepts me. When I am willing to love me and take care of myself, I no longer demand that someone else love me or take care of me. This does not mean that I don't want others to love me; it only means that I am not crushed when they don't.

Are you demanding that someone give you what you are unwilling to give yourself? Try giving to yourself what you really want or need. See if it is still so important that you receive it from someone else.

LIVING IN THE NOW

*Men spend their lives in anticipation,
in determining to be vastly happy
at some period or other, when they have time.
But the present time has
one advantage over all other; it is our own.*
Charles Caleb Cotton

I have known a great many troubles
but most of them never happened.
Mark Twain

During a telephone conversation my seventy-year-old mother said, "I just dread getting old more and more every day."

"Mom," I replied, "you are living getting old twice. Once when you get there, and once now."

Thoughtfully she said, "I guess you are right."

I suggested that once was enough, that she could deal with being old when it happened.

When my boys were younger, we frequently got into discussions about what they were going to do when they were in high school. Some of their ideas made me panic, and I tended to start my standard lecture. I finally realized I was crossing bridges before I came to them.

Once I came to that realization I responded to their "When I'm in the tenth grade . . . " with, "If you still want to do that when you get to the tenth grade, we'll talk about it then." It was amazing how much that reduced my anxiety and eliminated a lot of unnecessary discussion.

We create our own anxieties by trying to live our future now. We do that by playing "What if": What if we have a war? What if we have a depression? What if there's a hurricane? What if I lose this contract?

When we give up this game and live today today, peace and tranquillity return. We can still have long-range goals and plans for our future. We simply do today's work toward their achievement.

Are you playing the "What if" game and trying to live your future today?

We cannot know our future, but we can surely destroy our present by dwelling on our past.
Author unknown

A common game we can play to spoil our here and now is the game called "If only."

Linda was in a deep state of depression. She sat in my office playing this game: If only she had been a better mother her children would have turned out better... If only she had been a better wife she would not have lost her husband to another woman... Her list went on and on. She was immobilized by her guilt and self-hatred.

During our conversation she mentioned her religious faith several times. I asked her if her faith did not teach that she was forgiven for her mistakes. "Oh yes," she replied. "The Lord has forgiven me, but I haven't forgiven myself."

Very gently I took her by the hand and said, "When Linda is too good to forgive Linda, it really doesn't help to have a forgiving God." She stared at me in disbelief. "Linda," I continued, "you've been acting more righteous than God. He has forgiven you for being human and you haven't forgiven yourself. Did you know how to be a better wife and mother at the time?" She shook her head no. "Then of what are you guilty?"

Linda began to see that she had created her own hell. Before she left my office, she went through the process of forgiving herself. If there is anything you need to forgive yourself for, do it and move on.

Every time you hear yourself say, *"If only"* immediately replace it with, "That is history and it can't be undone. I choose to bring my mind back to present time."

The present time is the only time there is, so live it fully.

When it is time to die, let us not
discover that we have never lived.
Henry David Thoreau

Have you ever been driving and discovered that you have passed through some little town and not noticed it? That's what I call being unconscious. A lot of us go through the trip of life that way. We don't notice the little towns, we don't have any trouble along the road, and we don't experience the pleasure of the moment nor do we learn anything.

Years ago I saw a cartoon showing a grave marker with these words inscribed: "Here lies the body of John Doe, who died at the age of 39 and was buried at the age of 72." That cartoon spoke to me. Being unconscious is like walking around dead.

It is amazing how many things we can perform quite well while not being fully present. There is something wrong with this kind of unconsciousness; we fail to use our inner resources and miss a lot of experiences. For instance, have you ever eaten a meal and left the table feeling unsatisfied? You probably weren't present when you ate. Being conscious means being present in the moment. That is how we experience our experiences.

Experiment with your next meal. First really look at it. Experience your food with your eyes. Then smell it. What does it smell like? Now taste it. Chew each bite several times and notice how the flavor increases. Savor it. Enjoy it. Notice the pleasure you derive from the food. See if you need as much food as usual to feel satisfied. Did eating consciously make a difference?

All of us are challenged to keep our mind in present time. I still act unconsciously a lot. When I notice I'm doing it, I remind myself to come back to the moment. As you focus your mind on the present, notice how rapidly you expand your awareness. You can even hear what another is actually saying, rather than assuming what you are hearing is the same as what was previously said. As you practice staying present, pay attention to the difference in the quality of your work and improved relationships.

The danger of the past was that men became slaves.
The danger of the future is that men become robots.
Erich Fromm

Our biggest limitation in life is lack of awareness. Any thing we are not aware of, we don't have access to. Nothing can serve us until we know it is there. Awareness is a key to growth and power. To raise your awareness, create an imaginary observatory in your head. Observe both your inner and outer worlds. Start using the word observe in you conversation so that your mind will keep hearing the directive. Concentrate on being aware, ask your self, "What am I aware of?" That question will turn on the equipment in your observatory. It allows you to see things objectively and raises your awareness level.

Traveling to a nearby city to conduct a workshop, I observed men in the field harvesting maize. I became aware of the thought, "I know all about maize." The observer in me said, "What do you know?"

Startled and stammering, I replied, "Daddy raised maize when I was a little girl. The men itched a lot during harvest. We fed it to the chickens." That was all I knew. A few minutes before my thought had been, "I know all about maize." My familiarity with maize had made me think I knew all about it. Laughing, I began to wonder in how many other aspects of my life I thought I "knew all about" simply because I was familiar with it. Learning more about maize did not change my life; seeing the difference between familiarity and knowing did.

Developing the observant mind can help you in so many ways. After I had gotten the message of my son's accidental death, I was on the plane to where he was. I was in a state of shock, and devastation. Although I hurt with a depth I could not fathom, the observer part of me noted my pain and I became aware there was another part of me still intact and I would survive it.

Do you want to raise your awareness? Create an imaginary observatory and imagine a part of your mind as the observer. Then you can become both the observer and the participant.

Nothing is there to come, and nothing past,
but, an eternal now does always last.
Davideis

Ten-year-old Heather, with her freckles and big, brown eyes, sat across from me looking somewhat nervous. She was there because she was not doing well in school, although tests had shown that she was very bright. We talked for awhile about her school work and I told Heather I had a hunch about why she wasn't doing well. After a brief silence she asked what my hunch was. I said, "My hunch is that your body goes to school every day and your mind goes someplace else."

She lit up like a light bulb and said, "I think you are right."

"Heather," I asked, "where does your mind go?" She rolled her eyes around and said, "It goes home."

I then asked her to close her eyes and imagine her body sitting in a classroom without a mind. A minute later she opened her eyes and said, "That's awful."

Again I asked her to close her eyes, and this time to imagine her mind at home without a body. Her eyes popped wide open and she exclaimed, "I've been splitting myself up!"

I directed her to close her eyes again and this time to imagine going after her mind and bringing it back to where her body was. "That feels so much better," she said.

"Your mind will probably continue to run off Heather. Every time it does, go get it and bring it back to where your body is. Experiment with this for two weeks, then call and let me know if it made a difference."

At the end of two weeks I received her call. Enthusiastically she told me, "Boy, does my mind run off a lot! I had to go get it all week. It really made a difference—I made 95s, 98s, and a 100."

Keeping our mind in the present time is some of the hardest work we have to do. Heather is a nice reminder of the benefits of doing so, and the way to do so is by keeping our mind where our body is.

MINDING YOUR ATTITUDES

*The greatest revolution of our generation is the
discovery that human beings,
by changing the inner attitudes of their minds,
can change the outer aspect of their lives.*
William James

*As the plant springs from, and could not be without,
the seed, so every act of a man spring from the hidden seeds
of thought and could not have appeared without them.*
James Allen

One of the things I learned growing up on a farm is that you can't plant corn and get okra. When you want corn you plant corn; when you want okra you plant okra. That is the law governing seeds and the soil.

The law governing the mind works the same way. Thoughts and images work like seeds and the mind works like soil. Inspirations and conceptions held in focus begin to germinate, take root, and grow into reality.

Years ago I had a secretary who was on a weight-loss diet. Frequently I would hear her say, "I'm just a little fatty."

After three weeks of the diet she complained to me one day that she had lost very little weight. I asked her if she really wanted to lose weight.

Shocked, she blurted out, "Of course I do! Why do you think I'm on this diet?"

"Kathy, I hear you say to yourself several times a day, 'I'm just a little fatty.' You are giving your subconscious mind two instructions. One to lose weight, one to stay fat. In addition to your diet, you might want to start planting thoughts of slimness."

She agreed to experiment with thinking slim and imagining herself weighing her ideal weight. The following week she reported losing four pounds.

When we don't plant what we want to grow there in our minds, like soil, it will grow what blows there. When someone blows a negative remark your way make sure it doesn't land in your soil and grow there. Say to yourself, "Bad seed, I give it no power to grow here."

Our mind is a marvelous enabler when we are clear and plant the ideas and images that we want it to produce.

What kind of thoughts and images are you planting in your mind?

*The mind is its own place, and in itself can
make a heaven of hell, a hell of heaven.*
John Milton

One night I turned on the TV to a late-night talk show and there, being interviewed, was the renowned family therapist, Virginia Satir. She made the statement that one of the attributes of the mind is that it cannot stand not knowing. So when it doesn't know something, it makes things up.

I was fascinated by this idea and began to check my thoughts. It didn't take me long to observe the truth of her remarks.

One of my treasured relationships had been somewhat strained for some time. I sent my friend a note inviting her to lunch. Two weeks went by with no acknowledgment. I kept wanting to make things up about why I had not heard from her. What I seemed to make up was not complimentary to me or to her. When I noticed that I was doing this, I announced to myself that I was making up reasons and that the truth was that I did not know why I had not heard from her.

Finally I received a note from my friend. She was in another state, dealing with a serious illness in her family. Nothing I had wanted to make up was even close to the truth. That was a valuable lesson.

Some of the beliefs governing our life today were formed when we made things up because of limited understanding as children. Beliefs like," Everyone must like me in order to be okay." Iris was twelve years old when her mother and daddy were divorcing. She said to me, "It's my fault. I should have been able to do something." She made up that some how she was responsible because of her lack of understanding. The list goes on and on.

One of our biggest challenges is to uncover all that we've made up and not make up anything new. When we become aware that we are making something up, say to yourself, "You really don't know what the truth is, so don't make anything up, wait and get the facts."

Allow your self to become aware when your wonderful, curious mind is making things up, and wait until you know the truth.

Compared to what we ought to be, we are only half awake.
We are making use of only a small part of
our physical and mental resources.
William James

When I started out in the motivational business, most authorities agreed that we used between 10 and 15 percent of our potential. Jean Houston of the Mind Research Center in New York has stated that the average person uses no more than 10 percent of their physical potential and 5 percent of their mental potential. That's not very much considering that we have 90 to 95 percent sitting there unused. I began to ask myself, "If that is the case, why is it so?" I came up with several possible reasons.

Some of us don't want to be different. Our need for acceptance and approval is one reason we don't explore our possibilities. This is one of the most common denominators I find in working with people in the business place. When I am working as a coach, this is what I hear quite often, "I want everyone to like me." It is hard to be the boss and do the necessary things when we need approval. An old saying, "I don't even like you, yet I need your approval" comes to mind when I hear this admission.

Another reason we do not use our potential could be that we don't know that it exists. We don't really know what we are capable of until we are called upon to use it. In time of dire need, people have done extraordinary things such as lifting a heavy automobile off a child trapped underneath.

Also, we don't really need to use more of our potential to survive. Most of us are "getting along" just fine the way we are.

Psychologist Fritz Perls thought that the main reason we don't use our potential is that we get stuck in our old habits of thinking and reacting. I suspect that is indeed the case.

Every expert agrees that we all have much more potential than we are utilizing. What would you like to do that would challenge you to develop even more of your possibilities? Dream your dreams, then act as though you cannot fail.

*I've known countless people who were
reservoirs of learning yet never had a thought.*
Wilson Mizner

Many of us were taught what to think, and not to question. As a result, some have not learned to think for themselves. When this happens we become compliant, obedient, and fearful of forming or expressing our own opinions. As we mature, we begin to give ourselves permission to think.

Believing there is a core being within each of us with clear perception, we can expand our ability to think by questioning: Is there another way to look at this? In what other ways can this be so? How else can this be viewed? These kind of questions begin to open the mind.

To further this exercise, imagine yourself as an impartial witness to the situation. Your function is to stay open and gather data. Envision the situation or point in question in the center of a large room. You are walking around the concern in a full circle, seeing it from a series of different perspectives. Practicing this exercise as an objective observer allows you to expand your perspective and awareness.

There are people so afraid of responsibility they would rather accept the limitations of other people's thinking than think for themselves. After all, they could be wrong. Yes, and you could be right and they are wrong. Are you willing to trust yourself enough to think for yourself?

Speak the affirmative; emphasize your choice
by utter ignoring of all that you reject.
Ralph Waldo Emerson

The man's voice on the cassette tape was giving instructions on how to develop both sides of the brain. With my eyes closed I was focusing on following his directions. At one point he told the listener to focus on the right side of the brain and not to think about the left side. Until he instructed me not to think about the left half of my brain, I was not even conscious of having one. Once he had told me not to think about it, the left side dominated my consciousness.

Does this remind you of all the times you have said, "I am not going to do that again?" You were really determined not to repeat an act and then went back and did it again.

Instructing our minds not to think certain thoughts any more never works. You may even instruct yourself never to behave a certain way again only to find yourself repeating the familiar pattern. A young man said in class, "My goal is to handle my anger like a mature man." "What a worthy goal," I responded, "How does a mature man handle his anger?"

"I don't know," he replied. And that is why he didn't do it. We must replace old patterns of thinking and behaving with new, more desirable patterns. When our mind does not know what we want, it doesn't know what to do.

Changing behavior and attitudes is the same way. When our attention is focused on negative behaviors or attitudes, that is what we continue to experience. When our focus shifts from the undesirable to the desirable, we start experiencing new, more effective behaviors and attitudes. We erase by replacing.

Do you want to change an old pattern? Decide on a new one. Imagine yourself achieving the desired results, and then watch the desired future come into being.

Success doesn't come to you. You go to it.
You don't buy it with Green Stamps.
There is no paycheck until the work is done.
Marva Collins

In my classes I ask the question, "How many of you have been told that all you have to do is believe?" The majority of the hands go up. The next question is, "Has it worked?" And the answer is no. When we think that all we have to do is believe, we "fold up our wings" and wait for something to happen.

Many experts teach the value of good nutrition. Most of us believe good nutrition is essential to good health. Believing in good nutrition while eating junk foods does not make our bodies healthy.

Other experts preach the value of exercise. After listening to these authorities and looking at their evidence, most of us believe in the value of exercise. However, believing in exercise will not help the shape of our bodies, our energy level, or our cardiovascular system. Until we "get off our duff" and get our bodies moving, the belief will not make a difference.

We have many beliefs about ourselves, life, other people, and God. Some of these beliefs are valid, some are not. Belief is essential in a lot of things. Alone it is not enough. Action is also necessary.

Belief opens the door to possibility. Action takes us through.

Liberty of thought is the life of the soul.
Voltaire

While I was going through one of the more difficult times in my life, I was employed by a business college. One morning my supervisor said to me, "Bobbi, I don't know how you maintain such a good attitude under your present circumstances."

"It's simple," I said. "Every morning when I get up I say to myself, 'You have a choice. You can let this get you down, or you can rise above it.' "

"When you put it that way," he said, "you don't have much of a choice."

"When I put it that way, it is easy to choose."

Man's Search for Meaning, by Viktor E. Frankl taught me about choices. From him I learned that my right to choose is the only thing in life that cannot be taken from me. I did not always know about choices and I consider Frankl's lesson one of the most valuable I have ever learned. Giving myself choices, even in insignificant matters, makes a difference. For instance, one inner dialogue I have goes like this: "You can enjoy the pleasure of this pie for ten minutes, and then feel lazy and fat, or you can do something else pleasurable to keep your mind off the pie and keep yourself feeling good." Decisions become easier when the choices are clear.

When Al enrolled in my class he had been miserably unhappy for a number of years. After a discussion about choices Al came back the following week as excited as a small boy on Christmas morning. He eagerly reported how learning about choices had turned his life around. By giving himself a conscious choice in every situation he had turned his work environment into a happy, productive place for both himself and his employees. He said, "It's amazing how something so simple is so powerful!"

Look for your choices in your life.

Experience is not what happens to a man.
It is what a man does with what happens to him.
Aldous Huxley

At a small dinner party one night the conversation turned toward fasting. Three people at the table practiced fasting on a fairly regular basis, and they were all expounding on what they perceived as its benefits. After this discussion had gone on for awhile one of the men said, "I went nine days without any food while I was in Korea, and I certainly don't ever want to do that again."

I thought about that statement for quite some time. I remembered the times I had to miss a meal for some reason or another and how I had reacted. I usually felt very deprived, physically weak, and really hungry by the time of the next meal. Then I thought about the times I chose to skip a meal—or meals—when on a fast, and how differently I felt, both mentally and physically.

Having to go without food and choosing to go without food are entirely different experiences. I've thought about this often since then and observed how true it is in all facets of our lives. When we "have to" to do something, it becomes a burden and our energy is down. When we "choose to" do the same thing, our energy level goes up.

How about you? Do you have any "I have to" that you can change into an, "I choose to"? I bet you'll be surprised at the resulting difference in your energy level.

*Judgments are our personal
ego reactions to the sights,
sounds, feelings and thoughts
within our experiences.*
W. Timothy Gallwey

A number of years ago I read a book listing words that were judgmental. I was surprised at how many of them I was making without realizing it. That discovery really motivated me to think about the effects of making judgments. While progress has been slow, I've at least learned to recognize when I am doing it, and the consequences. Judgments block learning and acceptance of what exists. They even create emotional reactions that have their own consequences: Guilt, defensiveness, immobility.

To become nonjudgmental, as I've come to understand it, is to see clearly and add nothing to the facts. It does not mean ignoring flaws, errors, and mistakes; it simply means not adding anything to them.

I have been using the game of pool to observe my judgmental attitude. I make a shot, the ball goes where I want it, and I judge it to be a good shot. In the excitement of a "good" shot, I don't observe what I did so that I can repeat it. I make another shot, it misses the goal entirely, and I judge it to be a "bad" shot. Because of the judgment I don't observe what I did so as not to repeat it. A pool shot just is. The ball goes where I would like it to or it doesn't. If I am busy judging the action I'm not likely to find pleasure in the game or learn anything from it. This has been an enlightening experience and a pleasant way to work at being nonjudgmental (with the fringe benefit that my pool game is improving.) I am working to take this experience and apply it to myself, my job, and my relationships.

How do judgments affect you?

Perspective . . . use it or lose it.
Richard Bach

As an observer of human behavior, I find it interesting to see the different ways people react to the happenings in their lives. For example, I know two college students who both failed the same course. One student and her family reacted to this failure as though it were a catastrophe. Much of their mental and emotional energy was spent dwelling on how bad this was and how adversely it could affect her future. The other student regretted that he had not taken the course as seriously as he might have, and that as a result he was going to have to go to school during the summer to make it up.

One viewed the situation as catastrophic, the other as a passing inconvenience. As we reflect on things that have happened in the past, do we view events as catastrophes, when, in retrospect, they were merely passing inconveniences.

Now when I start getting uptight about things not happening the way I want them to, I'm learning to ask myself, "Will this be a catastrophe, or is it a passing inconvenience?" The tension subsides as I realize it is just an inconvenience.

How are you seeing the unwanted situations in your life—as catastrophes or passing inconveniences? It makes a difference in the quality of your living.

The ways in which a man accepts his fate
and all the suffering it entails . . .
1.gives him ample opportunity—
even under the most difficult circumstances—
to add deeper meaning to his life.
Viktor E. Frankl

While visiting a rehabilitation center for drug abusers, I met a young man named Adam.

"I really like your name."

He replied with a chip on his shoulder, "I don't know why, it just means dirt."

"Isn't that great!" I responded.

"You're kidding. What's good about dirt? Because of dirt I have to take baths and wash my hair and my clothes."

Remembering when I had first seen him, I said, "Adam, awhile ago I saw you walking around barefooted on the good green grass. I love to do that, too. We can do that because of dirt. Also, Adam, because of dirt we have all the beauty of nature, all the food we eat, and planet Earth on which to live." Adam looked at me, shocked: he had never thought about the good in dirt, and my hunch is he had not thought about the good in Adam, either.

Granted, when dirt is in the wrong place it can cause problems. However, the good it brings into our lives far outweighs the hassle. Which do you emphasize, the good or the trouble? They are both there. I have learned I that whatever we emphasize we multiply. I am not suggesting that you overlook the hassles in life. I am suggesting that you deal with them by emphasizing the good.

What have you been emphasizing?

*Everybody wants to understand painting. Why is there
no attempt to understand the song of birds?
Why does one love a night, a flower, everything that
surrounds a man, without trying to understand it all?*
Pablo Picasso

Ruth was really stuck. The course was nearly over and there was no evidence that she was making any progress. My plan was for her to come in to see me privately.

In telling her story she kept repeating over and over again that she did not understand why she wasn't getting ahead at work and why she was so very unhappy. She accompanied her drama with a sigh and shrug of the shoulders, as though she had given up.

"Ruth," I inquired, "do you think you have to understand what's happening to you before you can do anything about it?"

She repeated defensively, "I just don't understand how I've gotten myself into this mess."

My somewhat impatient reply was, "Ruth, do you have electricity in your house?" She nodded yes.

"Do you understand how electricity works?" She shook her head no.

"So you don't have to understand electricity to benefit from it. Ruth, insisting on understanding is a cop-out. I sense you are unwilling to do anything to make your life work."

I knew what Ruth was doing. When I did not want to experience life the way it was, I thought it to death trying to understand it. I shared this insight with Ruth. By the time she left she had decided on a plan of action.

Yes, I still like to understand, but understanding doesn't change the facts or circumstances. Are you too stuck in the need to understand something instead of determining what action needs to be taken to solve the problem?

*If there was nothing wrong in the world
there wouldn't be anything for us to do.*
George Bernard Shaw

A young girl whose father had recently died was sharing with me some of her anger about this loss. She ended by saying, "It just isn't fair." I agreed with her that she had gotten a rotten deal. I could see how hard it would be to lose a father at an age when you really needed him. The girl kept repeating, "It's just not fair." I asked her if she thought life was supposed to be fair, and she replied, "Yes, of course it is."

As gently as I could, I explained that I had lived for quite some time, and found that life was not always fair. For instance, was it fair for one person to be born with great mental ability so that learning came easily, while another person really had to work at it? We discussed this and other "injustices" that she had not considered. She acknowledged that she could see it wasn't fair that in some ways she had so much and some of the kids in school had so little. I said, "Yes, and as you accept the fact that life isn't fair you can recover from your loss."

Sometimes life deals us a rather difficult hand—a hand that truly seems unfair. When this happens, it is up to us to decide how we are going to react and how we will play out the hand. We can walk around shaking our head and saying, "It's just not fair," or we can take the hand we've got, get on with the process of living, and perhaps pick up some wild cards along the way.

How are you playing the hand life has dealt you?

God grant me the serenity to accept the things
I cannot change, courage to change the things I can,
and wisdom to know the difference.
Serenity Prayer

Why. It's a small three-letter word, and when it's used in the scientific and business world it can lead to the investigation of reasons or causes and promote discovery and creativity.

On the other hand, "why" as a constant approach to life can become immobilizing. Why me? Why did it happen? Why did they do that? These kinds of questions reflect an attitude that keeps a person trapped inside a problem.

I am chagrined to admit how much of a "why" person I was until a friend got my attention by telling me that asking why all the time was a waste of effort. Stunned into silence, I did a lot of thinking about "why." I realized that when we don't want to face reality and deal with life on it's own terms, we ask why things are the way they are. Asking why is usually a way to avoid accepting what is.

Face facts by asking "How can I deal with this? What can I do about it? Where can I find the solution? When am I going to do something about it?"

"Why" keeps us bound up in a problem or a situation. How, what, where, or when lead us toward a solution.

UNDERSTANDING YOURSELF

*The only conquests which are permanent
and leave no regrets are our conquests over ourselves.*
Napoleon Bonaparte

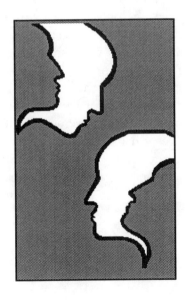

There is properly no history;
Only biography.
Ralph Waldo Emerson

History became interesting to me when I began to study the human nature behind events. Since human nature doesn't seem to be changing very much, history keeps repeating itself. And until we start to learn from history, I suspect it will continue to repeat itself just as we, as people, continue to repeat our life patterns.

A young mother I know kept herself upset. Much to her embarrassment, she cried when crying wasn't appropriate and experienced a lot of anxiety. I suggested that she keep a journal for a week and record all the events in her life and the feelings that accompanied them.

Together we went over her journal and discovered that she never stayed present in a single situation. When something started happening she had mentally already gone on to the next event. She came to realize that the attitude underlying this behavior was her sense that she had to hurry up or she would not get through with her daily work. As we studied her history, she realized that she had felt hurried ever since she was a child. This awareness helped her concentrate on staying in the here and now, and she began to change the course of her life.

A student of mine had recently gone through a divorce. Her most frequent complaint against her former husband was his self-pity. I watched her interest develop in another man; he got her attention by getting her sympathy. It is common for a person to marry someone with qualities similar to those of a former spouse. Until we study our lives and look at our own responsibility in shaping it we will probably continue to repeat the same scenes with new characters.

By studying our own biography, we can free ourselves to change our life patterns. Have you noticed your history repeating itself?

I will not be concerned at other men's not knowing me;
I will be concerned at my own want of ability.
Confucius

Pat, a sixteen-year-old girl who had run away from home a week earlier, was seeking a way to return home—and save face.

She sat before me pouring out all her reasons for leaving home. Then she concluded, "They just don't understand me."

"Pat," I responded, "it sounds to me as if you don't understand yourself. Do you?"

"No, I don't," she replied.

Gently I asked, "Pat, if you don't understand yourself, how can you expect your parents to understand you?"

She thought about that for awhile.

"Pat," I said, "I've discovered that occasionally other people know us even better than we know ourselves. There are parts of us that only we can know. There are parts of us that others can see that we don't recognize: And there is a part of us that is simply unknown.

What Pat needed was self-understanding. That takes time and effort. A good way to start is to listen to your own thoughts and feelings and to observe your own behavior. Listen to others carefully to see if they can be a mirror for you, show you a part of yourself that you have not recognized. Consider their opinions and try to notice if there is any truth in them. This can get you started knowing and understanding yourself. As you come to understand yourself, it won't be so important that anyone else does.

Have you been seeking understanding from the wrong source?

-87-

*Our opinion of people depends less upon what
we see in them than upon what they make us see in ourselves.*
Sara Grand

In psychiatry, projection is the unconscious act of ascribing to others our own ideas or impulses. We tend to assign to others both our negative and positive characteristics.

A young college student told me how the men she met were always letting her down. I asked how they were doing that. As she talked, we discovered that she formed a romantic, idealistic picture of each man. After some time, when she discovered he didn't conform to the image she had constructed, she blamed him rather than looking at how she had set him—and herself—up.

When we have traits that don't fit our concepts of ourselves, we sometimes deny them in ourselves and assign them to others.

When Wanda was in her graduate counseling program, she got very angry and impatient working with clients who had addictions to alcohol and drugs. Her supervisor asked her what her addiction was. With indignation she replied, "I don't have any."

Later Wanda was able to recognize that her anger and impatience were rooted in her addiction to food. She had put on forty pounds since her husband's death. When she acknowledged her addiction, she found that she could work with her clients more easily.

Without exception, every trait that has ever bothered me about someone else, I possess. It usually takes me awhile to admit it. Once I do, and I start to change this, the other person doesn't bother me anymore.

Do you want self-understanding? Allow others to be your mirror.

Sickness is a kind of warfare within the body;
Health the result of peace within our beings.
Dr. David Seabury

After scheduling time off from work and reserving a place to write, I was very disappointed to awaken ill during my first night at my retreat. My entire upper respiratory system was affected.

For two days I merely existed. Truly believing that every illness contains a message and that sickness can be a result of internal war, I began looking for conflicts. It didn't take me long to find them. The previous week had been an unusually hectic one. Knowing I would be out of my office several weeks, I had been torn much of the time between what I could get done and what there was to do. Perhaps that same conflict sometimes causes you stress too.

Jennifer's conflict showed up as periodontal disease. As her dentist began to question her about what had been so stressful that it had brought on this disease so suddenly. She revealed she was having an affair with her minister. Interestingly enough, his conflict showed up as pancreatic disease. Each was in conflict with their values which created enough stress to develop a disease.

The more serious the conflict, the greater the stress level we create. Do you ever feel torn by conflicting desires? Resolve them before "disease" sets in.

The tyranny of the "shoulds" and "oughts"
are a weight to carry. They take the joy
out of life and create unwarranted guilt.

We are handicapped by what we think we can't do.
Mark Twain

Our feelings of inferiority and inadequacy started with the S.O.B.'s that we grew up with: the shoulds, oughts, and buts.

When we were little people, our parents and the others who loved us wanted what was "best for us," so they told us we should do this and we ought to do that; we shouldn't do this and we ought not to do that. Naturally we believed them.

After awhile the shoulds and oughts became "the truth," and we, too, began to lay them on ourselves and others. These shoulds and oughts formed the ideal pictures of how we are supposed to be. When we did not fit our parents' ideal pictures, we sometimes received these messages: "I love you, but"; "That is really good, but"; "You are a neat person, but . . . " We began to develop the idea of conditional love and acceptance, and we began to feel inadequate and inferior.

As adults we still find that others have ideal images of us. We can react by getting angry because they "shoulded" on us. Or we can be even more irrational and feel inadequate and inferior because we don't fit their ideal pictures. Another option we have is to recognize that other people are imposing their images on us. We can let it be okay that they have a picture of us—and that we don't fit their images.

We must also recognize that we often impose these S.O.B.'s on others. Becoming aware that they are counter-productive burdens, we could decide to give them up.

We really can accomplish more and be more creative without them.

Every man has a rainy corner in his life
from which bad weather besets him.
Jean Paul Richter

One of the young men in a training seminar I was conducting for a large company came into class early. He began to tell me that both his parents were alcoholics. I suggested he stay after class that evening so that we could have a "pity party." I asked him if he had ever been to a pity party.

Blushing a bit he said, "Yes, but I had not recognized it before."

Another man in the class, a company comptroller, told me about his early background. His parents were extremely poor and he had not learned any of the social niceties or had any of the cultural advantages that his position demanded. He told me that he could handle the job itself well; it was the social expectations that were immobilizing him. I invited him to join our pity party.

Both men stayed after class. I explained that to have a successful "pity party" all we had to do was really talk about how bad our lives were. None of us would give any advice or suggestions for making life any better; we would only offer pity.

While both men had seemed to have legitimate reasons for self-pity, it only took about forty-five minutes for them to recognize how useless it was. Both left the "party" with some ideas on how to get on with their lives.

Do you have reason for self-pity? Give yourself a good pity party, then get on with your life.

FEELING YOUR FEELINGS

*The door to the human heart can
be opened only from the inside.*
Author Unknown

*Emotions are always the result of a given
perception and interpretation.*
John Powell

Sara and Johnny are about two feet tall and from their perspective they live with parents who look like powerful giants. One of these giants is out of control, looks down at them, shaking a finger and says, "You make me so angry. You have really upset me." Consider the confusion Sara and Johnny must have felt when this adult blamed them for the parent's anger.

Unwittingly, by example, the parent is teaching the child to be responsible for other people's feelings or to blame others for what they feel. Neither assumption is valid. I encounter an inordinate number of people who do both; blame others for their feelings or carry a false sense of responsible for other people's feelings.

Either position keeps us from using our feeling nature as a guide. Our emotions are like a signal. They signal us when we are on track or off track. Our feelings let us know when all is well or we have a problem that needs to be addressed. When we can use our emotions as a signal, we learn to view them as neither good nor bad, right or wrong. Only behavior is good or bad, right or wrong. We can learn to feel our feelings and control our behavior.

Many of us do not have a model to help us understand that we are responsible for our own feelings. It's time to reeducate ourselves and claim our powerful emotional nature without judgement.

Consider our emotional nature as our sixth sense. We experience our outer world through our five senses, and our inner world through our feelings. For example, imagine you are awakened in the middle of the night by a very loud noise. Your first conscious reaction is fear. However, preceding the fear came the unconscious thought, "What is it?" When you determine the source of the noise and discover that it is not a threat, your fear dissipates. The fear is a direct sensory response to the thought, "What is it?"

Once we understand that feelings are a sensory response to thinking and the concept penetrates our unconscious mind, we can began to experience our feelings without judgement. You will be surprised at the new surge of energy and freedom you will feel.

Feelings are the experiences of our thinking, beliefs and perceptions of the external world. They are a *signal* to let us know when we need to make changes, have suffered a loss, or all is well. You can celebrate them all.

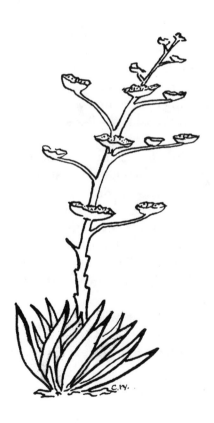

*Although the world is very full of suffering
it is also full of overcoming it.*
Helen Keller

Many of the men and women who participate in my classes have careers and are active in their communities in meaningful and rewarding ways. They are willing to take a lot of chances, and as a result they experience a lot of success. Paradoxically, these same people are sometimes emotional cowards, afraid to become involved because they think they will be hurt. When we experience this fear we are expressing an unconscious belief that in getting hurt we will be permanently harmed. As a result we are not really participating in intimate relationships; although we have surface relationships, we are afraid to get really close to others for fear we will be hurt. Those closest to us might die or leave us, for example.

I've had my share of deep hurts. At the time they felt as though they would last forever. I remember how losing someone important to me left me feeling a hole inside. Though I wouldn't have believed it at the time, the hurt was not permanent—nor was I harmed by it. It showed me everything was working right in my system. It is appropriate to hurt when we have any kind of loss. Hurt tells us how much we care, or how important the loss is to us.

Some hurts we experience for an unreasonable length of time because we keep rubbing salt into the wounds by reliving the experience over and over again in our minds. Sometimes we keep the wound open by insisting that it never should have happened. With no salt in the wound and acceptance of reality, wounds heal without any permanent damage.

Once we realize that we don't need to experience harm just because we have been hurt, we can open ourself up to genuine intimacy. As the thorn goes with the rose, pain sometimes goes with love. Loving again is the sure way to heal.

Are you willing to hurt when appropriate? If you're not, you will hurt permanently from loneliness. If you are, you are free to experience love and joy. Remember: You can experience hurt without being harmed.

I have always felt sorry for people afraid of feeling,
of sentimentality, who are unable to weep with their whole heart.
Because those who do not know how to weep
do not know how to laugh either.
Golda Meir

The daughter of a friend was describing some events in her life and some of her deepest feelings. As she related these experiences, I was moved to tears. This was a total shock to her. As I began to question her shock, she said to me, "You are strong and you have it together; you are not supposed to feel." Now it was my turn to be shocked. I acknowledged to her that I, too, considered myself a strong person and thought I "had it together" to some degree. I didn't see how that had anything to do with my ability to feel.

Since then a number of people have verbalized their belief that strong, successful people do not experience feelings like hurt and sadness. They think such feelings indicate weakness. Actually people who "have it together" have the same capacity to feel pain, sadness, or hurt as those who don't. In fact, one must have the capacity to experience pain in order to have the capacity to experience joy. What we feel is never a weakness, what we do about what we feel can be a sign of a weakness. The person who "has it together" may have the same feelings as the person who doesn't; he just handles his feelings differently. One handles them in a positive, constructive way, the other in a self-destructive way.

Your emotional nature is part of your *Being*. Your feelings serve as an asset, not something that must be repressed, denied, or allowed to run your life. There is never anything wrong with what you feel. You have enormous control and power over your emotional nature, and you don't have to let how you feel rule your behavior.

You may feel like kicking someone in the shins. That's okay. It's not okay to act on it. Our goal is to feel our feelings and control our behavior.

Anger ventilated often hurries towards forgiveness;
anger concealed often hardens into revenge.
Edward G. Buliver-Lytton

Gloria had gone through a divorce about two years before enrolling in one of my classes. She was still stuck in her anger and had not been able to put her life back together.

During her private time with me she said that she would like to tell her former husband the way she really felt.

"Sounds like you have not done that," I commented. I asked if she was ready to do it right then and there.

She hesitated, squirmed a bit, then said, "It wouldn't do any good."

"Yes, you are right, it will not change the facts, and it will do you some good to get it out of your system. This is a safe environment here and we are going to place this chair in front of you so you can imagine your former husband sitting there. You can tell him everything you have ever wanted to say. Call him anything you want."

With some prompting she began to verbalize all the hurt and anguish she had been experiencing. Between her sobs her voice rose to a high pitch of emotion. She vented her blame and self-pity. She called him a few choice names. When there was nothing left to say she looked at me with her eyes wide open and exclaimed, "I can't believe how good I feel!" Placing her hand over her chest she continued, "I have had a physical pain right here for months. I haven't been able to release it. Now it's gone. I don't understand how this has worked."

"You don't have to understand it because you have just experienced it. Just enjoy your freedom."

Feelings not expressed become an energy block in our bodies. Her former husband did not need to hear all of her emotions. However, she needed a safe place to express them for her release.

One of the greatest gifts we can give one another is to allow the other to express their deepest feelings without offering advice or judgement. Unfortunately, most listeners think they are supposed to "fix" them. But, the "fix" comes from healthy expression. If you are in relationship with a known fixer, before telling him how you feel, tell him you want to tell him how you feel and you aren't asking for advice or for him to make them different.

If you have been holding in feelings, find a willing listener and experience the release. If you find this process too uncomfortable write the feelings out and perhaps burn them up when you are ready to let them go. The important thing is get them out of your body.

*It is better by noble boldness to run the risk of being subject
to half of the evils we anticipate than to remain in cowardly
listlessness for fear of what may happen.*
Herodotus

A salesman I knew had an important client to call on, yet he kept putting off making the appointment. He told me that he had to develop better work habits. My hunch was that the problem wasn't poor work habits, rather it was fear of rejection by the important client that caused him to delay the call.

I asked him if he was afraid his client would say no. His response was, "I guess I am. I'm afraid he won't buy."

My next question was, "If he doesn't buy, will you feel rejected?"

"Yes," he responded, "I always feel rejected when people tell me no."

I then asked him, "Are they rejecting you or are they rejecting your service? There is a difference, you know." He looked surprised that there was a difference. He had been taking the rejection of his services as a personal rejection.

As I reflected on the incident later, I thought about all the things that never get said or done because of people's fear of rejection. When we realize that someone can say no to our requests, suggestions, or ideas and still say yes to us as people, maybe we will be willing to take more risks. Will you? Remember you say no occasionally yourself and it is perfectly ok. Everyone is not for everyone.

How much more grievous are the
consequences of anger than the causes of it.
Marcus Aurelius

A man named Joe was among my acquaintances. Joe was a man I really disliked. He was a very vindictive person who said things like, "I know that God says vengeance is His, but he needs me to help Him out." I shuddered when I heard that pronouncement and all his other declarations about how he was going to get even with various people. I really could not imagine myself as a vindictive person.

I thought my reaction to Joe was based on my strong belief about vindictiveness being a destructive way to deal with anger. Can you imagine my shock when I became aware that I was withholding love from a person because I felt he had caused me pain? My vindictiveness was so secretive that even I had not recognized it! Once I did, I decided to express my anger in an open and direct way that would allow our relationship to continue. When we don't have permission in our own minds to express anger directly, it takes other forms. Vindictiveness is one such form.

The healthiest thing we can do with our anger is to express it directly in a way not accusing or blaming the other person involved. It's *our* anger. We created it, so we need to express it, without blame.

It really is safe to express your anger, if you express it without attack or blame. People usually know we are angry anyway. Expressing it clears the air.

A splendid freedom awaits us when we realize that we need not feel like moral lepers or emotional pariahs because we have some aggressive, hostile thoughts and feelings toward ourselves and others. When we acknowledge these feelings we no longer have to pretend to be that which we are not.
Joshua Loth Liebman

Up until his dad's death the year before Mike had been a model student and had had good relationships both at home and at school. Since his father's death he had been in constant trouble. I had a hunch he was displacing his anger, so I "went fishing."

"Mike, if I were thirteen and my dad died when I needed him most, I would be mad."

"I am," he said, dropping his eyes and head, "but God took him."

"If God took my dad when I really needed him, I would be mad at God."

Barely whispering he said, "I am."

"Have you told God that you are mad at Him?"

"No, He would strike me dead."

"Mike, God already knows you are angry with Him and He understands. You just need to talk with Him about your anger so that you can get over it."

Like so many of us, Mike did not feel safe about being angry with God, so he displaced his anger. He considered it safe to act out his anger at school, where he didn't have as much to lose.

To everyone's relief, Mike was able to face and resolve his anger. His mother reported that he was soon his old self again.

Probably all of us know someone who is pleasant, kind, and considerate until he gets behind the wheel of an automobile. Then a personality change occurs; our mild-mannered friend curses out half the drivers on the road in language that is out of character.

Like Mike, this person doesn't think it is safe to be angry with whoever is the real target. So he directs his anger toward someone in whom he has no emotional stake. Are you displacing your anger, or handling it directly?

Hearing is one of the body's five senses.
But listening is an art.
Frank Tyger

While lunching with a friend one day I was conveying to her a very strong feeling about something that was going on in my life. She gazed into space and said, "I wonder what that is all about." I felt depersonalized, as if I were a problem in a textbook. The other feeling I had been discussing became secondary because at that moment I felt fury. I was glad that our lunch was almost over.

Determined to figure out why I felt such rage, I looked back at the history of our friendship. She had been a very supportive friend in many ways. She was someone I really cared about. As I began to study the relationship, I remembered the other times I had been just as furious with her. Each time it had happened when I was sharing my feelings. Her pattern was always to diagnose or analyze my feelings rather than to acknowledge them.

Aha! That was it. I did not want a diagnosis or analysis. I only wanted to share the feelings. Seeing my friend as a mirror, I promised myself that day that I would acknowledge people's feelings before I offered them anything else. I had experienced how important it was to be acknowledged and what it felt like when I wasn't.

On another occasion I was feeling down over a situation and related this feeling to a different friend. His response was, "That's kind of hard to take, isn't it?" All he did was acknowledge my feeling—and I felt release, and affirmation as a person.

Are you analyzing or acknowledging other people's feelings?

IMPROVING RELATIONSHIPS

*The meeting of two personalities is like the
contact of two chemical substances:
if there is any reaction, both are transformed.*
Carl Jung

Examine the contents, not the bottle.
The Talmud

Among those attending a weekend workshop I conducted for secondary educators were a priest and a nun, both dressed as laymen with nothing to set them apart physically from the group. I soon observed that some students in the group set them apart anyway.

On Friday I had spent quite a bit of time talking with the priest. He asked me if I had any trouble seeing him as a person. I smiled, because I understood his question, and said, "No, I'm aware of you as a human being. Having chosen to be a priest does not exclude you from the things that other people feel and experience." He told me how difficult it was for people to relate to him as a person; most related to him only in his role as a priest.

On Saturday I asked the sister if she had the same problem in her relationships with people. Pointing to a young man in the group, she said, "Oh yes. In fact, he can't stand my being here without my habit. He has expectations of what I'm supposed to do and say and how people should respond to me, and he becomes terribly upset when it doesn't work that way." She went on to say that wasn't unusual, and that it definitely was a problem.

Since then I've been reflecting on how we often put a person in a role and how we have certain expectations we associate with that role. Then we become upset or disappointed when he or she doesn't live up to it and fulfill those expectations. I see this most frequently in husband-and-wife roles, although it's really universal. How are you seeing and responding to others? In the role you have created for them, or as another human being?

Maturing is the process by which the individual
becomes conscious of the equal importance
of each of his fellow men.
Alvin Gaeser

At a party one night a woman came up to me and said she had been reading my newspaper column. Then she remarked, "You sure have a lot of interesting friends." Because of the way she said it, I wasn't sure if she believed they really existed. She was a somewhat older woman, and surprised me with her aliveness, vitality, and youthful enthusiasm. Before the evening was over, she became one of the interesting people I know.

Remembering this later and feeling very fortunate about my friends, I commented to someone on how lucky I was to have so many interesting people in my life. I just knew I was the luckiest person around. His response surprised me. He said, "Bobbi, the people you meet are the same people everyone else meets; people are interesting to you because you are interested in them."

This reminded me of the story about a man arriving in a new town who asked a local resident what kind of town it was. The wise resident replied by asking the newcomer how it was where he came from. The newcomer explained that he had found the people cold and unfriendly. The resident replied, "You'll find them the same way here." The resident knew that the man's attitudes would determine the way he saw others.

How are you experiencing the people who come into your life? Can you see each individual as someone unique and get to know how they think and feel without judgment? It is really quite interesting what you can learn. Sometimes this openness will bring you understanding, sometimes laughter, sometimes compassion.

*The deepest craving that we have
is the craving to be appreciated.*
William James

An attractive, well-groomed woman in her mid-forties sat in tears as she poured out her story. Her marriage was breaking up. It was obvious that she was in pain and that she did not want that to happen. She began to tell me what a terrific fellow her husband was. She recited a long list of his virtues and told me how much she admired and respected him. I could not see what had gone wrong, so I asked her.

She really broke down then and said, "All I've ever done is complain and find fault with him."

I asked her if she had ever told him that he was a terrific fellow.

"No," she replied, "I was afraid it would go to his head and he would leave me. If he knew how great he was, he sure wouldn't want me."

I sat for a moment stunned by her reasoning—or perhaps by the lack of it. Then I wondered how many people withhold genuine praise or appreciation for fear that it will "go to their head" and result in being rejected.

I noted that the woman's fault finding and criticism had obviously not worked. Since at this point she had nothing to lose, I suggested that she might want to go home and tell this "terrific fellow" the truth, exactly what he really did mean to her. She did, and they eventually worked out their problems.

A friend of mine reported he had a "very ugly" professor when he was in college. The professor had one of the most gorgeous wives my friend had ever seen. Not understanding how that could happen he went to the professor and said to him, "Prof, you are ugly. How did you attract such a beautiful wife?" I loved the professor's answer. "Well, he said, I know I am ugly. However, I love beauty and to have beauty around me, I knew I had to let her know how gorgeous she is. So, every morning, I tell her how beautiful she is and how lucky I am to have her in my life. She comes home every night to hear it again."

Do you ever withhold praise or appreciation? We need to learn from the professor. We all need acknowledgment, and we seek out people who will fill that need.

It is true I am only one, but I am one.
And the fact that I cannot do everything
will not prevent me from doing what I can do.
Edward Hale

My father developed lung cancer and his dying was slow and painful. I was both stunned and baffled as I watched his body deteriorate while his attitude and spirits steadily improved. Never once did he complain. Astonishing! When asked how he was doing, he always answered, sometimes with great effort, "I'm better."

As I studied my Dad's response, I was puzzled. There was no way he could be better. One day, I got him aside and said to him, "Dad, I want to know what this has been like for you." He looked down at the floor for a minute, then he looked me straight in the eye and said, "To tell you the truth, it has been good." He was happy as he began to enumerate all the people who had been to see him and what each had done for him.

His attitude became clear. I remembered the trauma of his childhood. As a young child he had polio and required much attention. His mother, being young and burdened with his care, had instilled guilt by telling him, "You owe me Albert, because you were so much trouble." Unfortunately, she never got over that mindset. As a result, I suspect, on a deep level, he had not felt loved or valued for being himself.

As Dad's illness progressed, people came from far and near to be with him. Through the experience of their love, the soul of the wounded child within him was validated and healed. Indeed, he was better. How simple, yet paradoxical. In the process of dying, he was healed.

We don't have to be dying to need small acts of love and acknowledgment, nor do we need to wait for a crisis in another's life to give the gift of love and acknowledgment.

*Love consists in this, that two solitudes
protect and touch and greet each other.*
Rainer Maria Rilke

While visiting another city, I met a woman who seemed to have everything going for her. She was attractive and talented, with a charming home and what seemed to be a stable family life. She was also extremely depressed and unhappy in her marriage. She told me how she and her husband had met, how they had cared for each other, and how they used to be able to talk for hours. As she described the way they were when they had met eight years before, they both sounded like really exciting, vibrant, fun-to-be with people. As she described her husband now, he didn't sound very interesting, and certainly not exciting. And as I listened to her complain, it was obvious that she, likewise, wasn't either.

I offered a suggestion as to what she might do to revitalize the relationship. Her response was, "I have my pride."

Driving back to Corpus Christi I was reflecting upon this comment when I realized that it's generally not the "other woman" or the "other man" that is a threat to a marriage; it's boredom, and apathy. I asked myself, "If I were my mate, would I want to come home to me? Would I find me interesting, exciting, or even pleasant to live with?" These questions jolted me into seeing my responsibility in a relationship. I hope they are enlightening to you as well.

Unless you give up your resentment
to your parents you remain as a child
Fritz Perls

A woman was leaving class one night when she turned at the door and said, "I am forty-eight years old and I recognized for the first time tonight that I am still trying to get my mother's approval."

During another discussion a young woman described how much her mother's expectations had influenced her feelings of low self-esteem. Everything her mother had said might have been proclaimed as a fact by God himself, they were so influential.

In his book The Language of Feelings, Dr. David Viscott states that "Parents are simply people who happen to have children." I have thought about that statement a lot, and I shared it with the young woman. I asked what her attitude would be if she looked at her mother as an equal, a person just like herself, rather than as her mother. She thought about that very carefully and replied, "Really very different. As a person, I could see her with understanding and acceptance." I suggested that she might want to experiment with seeing her mother as an equal for awhile and see if their relationship changed.

As children we see our parents as omnipotent, all-knowing and all-wise. If they fail us, we think they have done it deliberately. We don't see their humanness, the limits of their wisdom, their insecurities, or their pain. Often we carry this attitude into our adult lives. Becoming conscious of the humanness of my parents has caused me to view them as people who have had to deal with their own experiences, their triumphs and failures. This realization has allowed my expectations of them to fall away, along with the expectations I held for myself as a parent.

I have come to realize that while parents have high expectations of their children, it is nothing compared to the expectations children have of their parents. How about you? How are you seeing your parents, and how is that view affecting your life?

We are all so much together,
but we are dying of loneliness.
Albert Schweitzer

Have you ever been together with someone and yet not really been together? I'm sure we've all had that experience. The sad thing is that for some people this is a way of life. They share the same space, eat at the same table, and never tune into each other.

Carolyn was suffering from emotional malnutrition. Her husband was a highly successful corporate executive who worked ten hours a day. When he came home he would eat, discuss business, and then go to his study to read so that he could keep current on business and world affairs. His withdrawal caused Carolyn to withdraw also. As I gathered information about their backgrounds it became clear to me that as children neither of them had adult models who knew how to be attuned to them. Not surprisingly they had not learned how to tune in to each other.

Togetherness is not achieved through quantity of time. It's achieved through quality of time. We have to change our self-concern to concern for another long enough to put ourselves in the other's place and give some evidence that we understand what they are experiencing. That's togetherness.

When we have experienced togetherness the result is a strong feeling of well-being. When someone has been very attuned to us and lets us know it, that creates music for our soul. We can experience warmth and closeness. It takes a lot of work, and it's worth every bit of the effort.

Are you being together with someone without really being together? Try tuning in.

The only thing we have to fear is fear itself
Franklin Delano Roosevelt

Along with all the pleasures that come from living in the beautiful "Sparkling City by the Sea" comes the threat of hurricanes. During one such threat, while the storm's exact destination was still unknown, I found it interesting to study human behavior under stress. I observed panic, fear, and conflict. Some people said they felt guilty for praying that the hurricane would go somewhere else. I also observed a growing communal closeness, supportiveness, helpfulness, and caring.

I myself felt calm in this time of possible threat, primarily because it was the first time I had ever charted the path of a hurricane on a weather map and listened to the official weather bulletins. Rumors of all sorts could be heard just about every place I went. Every time I heard a rumor like "It's coming here," I would go back and look at my map to see the direction the storm was actually traveling. I soon knew that it was not in fact moving in our direction.

As I reflected on what various people had told me the storm was going to do, I concluded that people often hear what they fear. As I thought about this, I realized that it is often true in personal relationships, too. People sometimes hear rejection from someone because they fear rejection. Some hear criticism when criticism isn't intended, because they fear criticism and can't deal with it.

What do you fear? Is there a real basis for it? How often do you actually experience what you fear? Could you have interpreted events to coincide with what you feared or expected? Consider that you could be hearing what you fear rather than what was meant.

You give but little when you give of your possessions.
It is when you give of yourself that you truly give.
Kahlil Gibran

A client who meets many people said to me, "When I meet these people again, they never recall meeting me." He was obviously distressed about not making a lasting impression. Some people have enrolled in my classes specifically because they want to be remembered by others and leave a favorable impression. I generally find that they themselves are very difficult to get to know. They want to be remembered, yet they haven't recognized that they must give of themselves in order to be remembered.

Several years ago I spent a weekend at a small resort with several people I had just met. After some close conversations we got to know each other well. One man began to relate some very personal conflicts with which he was struggling. As he told of his inner battles, our whole group felt warm and supportive. This sharing opened the door for the rest of us to reveal something of ourselves.

When Sunday evening came, none of us wanted to break the closeness and go our separate ways. Reflecting on the weekend I marvel at how near we all felt, simply because we were willing to share of ourselves and our inner worlds. It is not likely that we will ever forget one another.

The people I do forget are the people I never really get to know. Do you want to be remembered? Try revealing a part of yourself.

*I have never met an aggressive person
who wasn't a fearful person.*
John Bradshaw

Our greatest pain results in holding the belief that something is wrong with us when we are not loved by the person we want to love us. Jim was a young man who said to me, "I don't know what is wrong with me. My dad loves my sister, but he doesn't love me." How sad that he failed to recognize not getting the love in a way he desired did not mean something was wrong with him. Jim had not considered the possibility that his dad was too wounded to love him the way he needed to be loved.

Ellen was in love with a man who had no ability to be faithful to one woman. She said to him one day, "Why am I not enough for you?" With all the man's flaws, he had the good sense to say to her, "Ellen, you are too smart for this. This is my problem and it has nothing to do with you." All of us need to realize we are loved or not loved by another depending on that individual's ability to love. The evidence of this lies in observing people who love even mean and obnoxious characters.

Georgiana related to me how much of a failure she was as a wife. Her husband was very critical of all she did and was unhappy with her most of the time. I inquired how her husband got along with the rest of his family and in his business. It became obvious that she wasn't the only one who could not please him.

"Do you feel personally responsible for your husband's unhappiness?"

"Yes, how else can I take it? He says it's my fault."

"Didn't you say your husband wasn't speaking to several members of his family?" She nodded. "You also said he had trouble keeping good employees because of the way he treated them." Again she nodded in agreement. "It appears to me that your husband is unhappy in most of his relationships. If that is so, I don't think you have to take his unhappiness personally."

All three of these people gave other people the power to define their lovability. This is a sure way to get our cookies crumbled. When we are tempted to do that remember, "How people treat you is a statement about them not you!"

*Other peoples opinion of me
is none of my business.*
Unknown

Audiences all across the country raise their hands when I ask the question, "How many of you take things personally?" Taking things personally seems to be the most common form of self-induced suffering. Why it is such a common practice is a mystery, unless Dr. Carolyn Myss is correct when she suggests we only know how to bond with another through our suffering.

If you are willing to find a healthier way to relate to others, I will tell you how to stop taking things personally. There are two phrases you will want to eliminate from your vocabulary. They are, "to me" and "on me." These phrases indicate you have internalized another's behavior. Here are examples of how we do this: "Do you know what she did *to me?*" " Let me tell you what he said *to me.*" "He died *on me.*"

Let's separate the facts from the internalization that something was done *to us.* By adding a period after the facts, and dropping the *to me's* and *on me's,* we can be objective about what happened. Frankly, people do what people do because that is the way they are. You will not get your feelings hurt nearly so often when you realize that how people treat you is a statement about them, not you. How you handle their treatment is a statement about you

Once you are able to let go of the lie you tell yourself, that *it's always your fault,* then you become detached and see other people's behavior objectively. So the next time someone tries to crumble your cookies, say to yourself, "That is about them, not about me!" And choose your behavior with your new insight accordingly. Remember, when the boss is yelling and out of control, that is about him and you can stay detached. Observing how people treat others is a great way to get to know them and to understand more about yourself from your interaction with them.

*How People treat you
is a statement about them
not You!*

*How you handle it
is a statement
about you!*

I know you believe you understand what
you think I said, but I am not sure you
realize what you heard is not what I meant.
Author Unknown

In a workshop for communicators conducted by John Grinder and Judith Delozier I learned that their theory was, "There are no mistakes in communications, only outcomes." That was a rather profound statement the first time I heard it, and I've thought a great deal about it since.

One evening I was with a small group of women discussing some of the things that were said to us when we were younger and how we let them affect us. I remembered that when I was in the sixth grade my cousin was a substitute teacher for my class. I felt anxious to be good and wanted to impress her. However, when it was my time to read aloud, I read very poorly. When class was over she came up to me and said, "Bobbi, you really can't read very well, can you?"

In my mind the "voice of authority" had spoken, what she had said was fact. The outcome of that communication was that I became a non-reader. I read only what I had to until I was thirty years old. This was about the time I began reexamining and discarding some old programming. I discovered that I liked to read and since have become an avid reader.

What kind of outcomes do you want when you communicate? The desired outcomes motivate us to be more careful about the communication we send. If we are not getting the desired outcome, then we need to change the way we communicate. Before we speak, we need to ask ourselves, "What do I want to happen? Will my style of communication achieve the results I want?" We need to be responsible for the tone and the intent of the messages we send.

But, if I tell you who I am,
you may not like who I am,
and that's all that I have.
John Powell

Grace is a gorgeous, talented, and successful, young woman, Prominent both socially and professionally. She had just fallen, head over heels in love with her idea of Mr. Perfect.

She came to see me because she was scaring herself into believing she was going to lose him. I asked her on what she was basing her fear.

She said, "I've told him the truth about my insecurities. I don't wear my sophisticated and successful mask around him. I've told him what I really like and dislike, and even my self-doubts and insecurities."

"Grace, that is beautiful."

Tearfully she said, "Yes, but suppose that's not what he wants. What if he wants someone who is really sophisticated and self assured?"

"Grace, if you wore your mask and played a part, and he fell in love with the mask and role, would you ever feel totally loved?"

"Not really," she sobbed.

"You have taken a chance. If he loves the you that is, then you will truly feel loved. Are you willing to settle for less?"

Hesitantly she said, "I guess not, but it would sure hurt to lose him."

"Yes," I said, "and it would hurt more having him love what you are not."

To feel loved and accepted we must be willing to reveal our authentic self and make it safe for our partner to do the same.

Mistakes

Are like flats, Just Fix Them

LESSONS FROM EVERYDAY LIFE

The greatest, the most important of the arts is living.
Aldous Huxley

*If he is indeed wise he does not bid you to
enter the house of his wisdom, but rather leads
you to the threshold of your own mind.*
Kahlil Gibran

I remember a teacher who had a very positive influence in my life. Her "thing" was Chinese proverbs. Each day she had a new proverb on the board, and quite often we discussed the great truth it revealed.

My favorite—and the one I remember best—is this: "Give a man a fish and he eats today. Teach a man to fish, and he eats forever." As an educator I make an effort to keep this thought uppermost in my mind. If I give all the answers, supply all the needs, I'm keeping the student dependent upon me. I really have faith that all people have within themselves everything they need to make their lives work. Conveying that faith and not giving a person the solutions to specific problems empowers the individual to find her own solution.

I had been talking with Sandra about her problem for about forty minutes. She kept asking, "What should I do?" Not having been successful in getting her to come up with her own solution, I suggested we switch roles. I would be the client. I would present my problem to her, and she could tell me how to handle it. In this role reversal she had an immediate solution. Her idea sounded like good advice to me, and I suggested that she take it. She left and we both felt good.

Many parents talk to me about their children. They say, "I've given them everything. I just don't understand why they won't do anything." Or "I've seen that they have everything they need. I just don't understand why they aren't motivated." Each time I hear these remarks I think, "Yes, you've given them fish, but have you taught them how to catch the fish?"

Are you giving away fish, or are you teaching people how to catch their own?

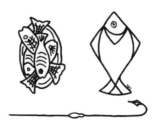

Every problem contains a gift.
Richard Bach

When I ask John, a friend of mine, how things are going in his life and he replies, "I've had quite a few learning experiences lately," I know he is dealing with some problems. I enjoy this friend because of the way he handles his problems. His philosophy is, "There are no problems, only learning opportunities." John has motivated me to take this positive approach to my own life.

When I say "problem" my body feels weary and my mind is focused on the negative. When I say "learning opportunities" my body feels excited and ready to go, and my mind is open and receptive. The results are very different. Looking back at my life my greatest growth has come about because of some problem that really did contain a learning opportunity.

Reflecting upon the value of problems, I remembered the naturalist who one day was watching a butterfly emerge from its cocoon. After watching the butterfly struggle for some time he decided to help it. He took out his knife and slit the cocoon enough for the butterfly to free itself. It fluttered around for a little while, then dropped to the ground, dead. You see, it is its struggle to gain freedom from the cocoon that helps the butterfly develop the strength necessary for flying.

Problems provide us with an opportunity to discover dormant talents and abilities of which we may be unaware. They contribute to our overall growth. How are you letting problems affect your life?

Time cools, time clarifies: no mood can be maintained
quite unaltered through the course of hours.
Thomas Mann

Have you ever been so happy and on such a natural high that you felt as though you could not contain yourself, and wonder how anyone could feel so good? It's a fantastic state to be in. When I am in this state, I tell myself to enjoy it for as long as it last.

Life has demonstrated to me that nothing is permanent. No state of being lasts forever. If I want to continue to be happy, I will have to work at it. This continuous state of change also helps me to be aware of the fact that painful feelings are not permanent either. I can remember a time in my life when I hurt all the way to the core of my being and felt as though I had no life left in me. At the time I couldn't imagine that ever changing. However, it did. It was not permanent either.

Are you suffering distressful emotions of any kind? Acknowledge the feelings. Allow yourself to really experience them, and at the same time remember that they are not permanent. Are you experiencing happiness, joy, excitement? Allow yourself to really enjoy the experiences and know that they, too, will not be permanent.

For everything you have missed,
you have gained something else:
and for everything you gain, you lose something.
Ralph Waldo Emerson

A friend once shared this philosophy with me: "You have to give up something in order to get something else." I had not heard that idea before. I thought about it for a few minutes and then dismissed it from my mind.

Later, as I was reaching for a second helping of ice-cream pie, her idea popped back into my mind. I realized how true her statement was in this instance; I had to give up that second helping of pie in order to maintain the weight I wanted. Then I began to reflect on other situations when we have to give up something in order to get something else. I could think of many instances when this idea applied to material things—like giving up the comfort of an old pair of shoes to have a more stylish pair, or trading in the old car we are still fond of to get a new model.

Though it was easy to see how the concept was applicable to the physical world, I began to wonder whether it also applied to emotional experiences. I thought about an acquaintance who had lost the love of her life. She was still holding on to that past experience. Until she could let it go, give it up, she would not be ready for a new love. We have to give up our resentments and hostilities to have peace and tranquillity. We give up despair to have hope, neutrality to have love, doubt to have faith, and on and on. What do you want in your life? Is there anything you need to give up in order to get it?

Affirmation of life is the spiritual act
by which man ceases to live unreflectively
and begins to devote himself to his life with
reverence in order to raise it to its true value.
To affirm life is to deepen, to make inward,
and to exalt the will to live.
Albert Schweitzer

Joy is one of the most alive people I know. Her eyes dance and she moves with enthusiasm. Occasionally she says, "Hooray for death!" I found her vivaciousness and that phrase incompatible. Each time I heard her say "Hooray for death!" I felt puzzled. Every time I heard the phrase I attempted to see what truth lay behind it. I could understand "Hooray for the afterlife," though I didn't feel too eager to rush the experience.

Finally I began to understand Joy's intense aliveness.

The concept of death makes us fully aware of life and of our strong desire to live. Thinking about our own death helps us to clarify our values. All too often we make time spent for tasks of greater importance than the time spent for making relationships; *doing* more important than *being*. We are believing in spirituality rather than making time for spirituality.

When a situation arises that we feel irritated about, we need to ask ourselves, "When life is over, is this going to matter?" If the answer is no, then we can let it go. If it was yes, then we need to put our energy into a solution. When we get upset and make a big deal of something, we need to ask ourselves, "When life is over and done, will this make a difference?" No. Hooray for death!

Frankly, we can amaze ourselves at how well we can survive without some things we once thought necessary, even without love from a person we had desperately wanted to love us. Hooray for life!

Although the day is coming to an end
I feel that I have conquered.
I look for strength for tomorrow so that I may start again.
Michael P. Fenton

A client was conferring with me about an employee who was behind in her work. My client, frustrated, said, "I've relieved her of phone duties, made sure she had no interruptions, and hired extra help so that she could get caught up. It has been two weeks and she is still not caught up."

Thinking about this situation, it dawned on me that the term caught up could have a negative connotation. What was going to happen to the employee when she got caught up? Would she be without anything to do? Would she be without a job? And, besides, was it really possible to get caught up? Each new day brings with it both new and repetitious work and new and old projects. That means there is always something to do.

I realized I, too, had been frustrated for years trying to get caught up. As I repeated the term caught up, I felt a tightness in my abdomen, a feeling of being hurried. I had felt hurried for years. Suddenly I felt a shift in my energy level when I realized that the worker, my client, and I had been hindered by our negative sensory response to the term caught up. Since my client and I both had busy and productive businesses, we wouldn't ever get caught up. There would always be work to do. However, we could get current and stay current. With getting current as my new aim my body felt suddenly relaxed. Using a different term to express my goal created a very different feeling.

My client, her employee, and I have lessened our frustration, and increased our satisfaction. By switching our objective from getting caught up which infers completion to staying current which infers ongoing.

It is only by risking our persons
from one hour to another
that we live at all.
William James

Imagine yourself invited to a magnificent banquet. It is the most elaborate banquet you will ever have the opportunity to attend. You groom yourself well and wear your finest clothes.

You arrive at the banquet hall. It is elaborately decorated, filled with magnificent arrangements of long-stemmed roses. You move from one arrangement to another to see how many varieties you recognize. As you examine a rose, you prick yourself on a thorn. Quickly you lose interest in the roses and move toward the banquet table.

You have never seen so much food in your whole life. Since you are a connoisseur of fine food, you are having a field day. You look at the first dish carefully and sample it sparingly to discern how it was prepared and what is in it. You check your analysis with someone who has just eaten and, sure enough, you were right. Feeling very pleased with yourself you move onto the next dish and repeat the process. You really do know as much about food as you thought!

The banquet is over and the guests are leaving. Now you realize that although you've had a great time nibbling and guessing the ingredients in each dish you have not eaten enough of anything to satisfy your hunger.

The banquet is life. Do you quickly turn away from the beauty if it gives you a little pain? Are you just studying it and analyzing it to death, or partaking of it and fully participating in it?

ACHIEVING YOUR GOALS

In the long run men hit only what they aim at.
Henry David Thoreau

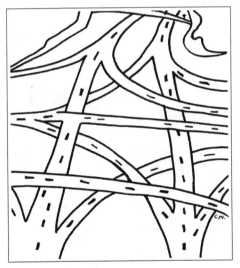

If you don't know where you are going,
you don't know which road to take.

To drift is to be in hell;
To be in heaven is to steer.
George Bernard Shaw

You have just heard that you have won a trip. You can go anyplace you choose. All expenses are paid.

The first thing you have to do is decide if you want to go. If you do, you will then need to decide where. The next decision is how and when you will travel. You will have to make decisions about packing and pocket money.

Most folks don't take trips without choosing where they want to go, getting clear directions on how to get there, and arranging reliable transportation. Yet these same people may never consider choosing where they want to go in life.

On our journey through life we take many trips and we need goals along the way. A goal gives us direction and keep us on the right track. Without them we don't know which road to take.

Have you noticed how many active people die soon after they retire? Is it possibly because they didn't plan a new road to go down? With nowhere to go, do they deteriorate and even die? When some people don't have anyplace to go they simply stay in bed in the morning or move through their days aimlessly.

Having goals is fundamental to everything we do. They are essential to our mental and emotional well-being. What the goals are is not as important as the fact that they exist. Goals give our lives meaning and purpose and help us choose the roads we want to travel. Even the achievement of daily goals and goals for each task enrich our lives and give us satisfaction and fulfillment.

Life can happen to you or you can happen to life by setting your goals and committing yourself to achieving them.

To think we are able is almost to be so;
to determine an attainment is frequently attainment itself.
Earnest resolution has often seemed to have
about it almost a savor of omnipotence.
S. Smiles

The day was almost gone and I was feeling frustrated because I had not accomplished much. As I reflected on what had gone amiss, it occurred to me that I had not accomplished anything because I had begun the day with nothing particular in mind to accomplish. It became clear that lacking instruction from me as to what I wanted, my mind didn't know what to do.

Without goals your mind is like a big jet plane all revved up with nowhere to go. Once the goal is established, the mind, like the jet plane, is ready and able to perform.

I had talked about writing this book for quite awhile and written a few essays from time to time. Once I gave myself a deadline to complete the book and made the commitment, I had given a clear directive to my subconscious.

Writing and choosing an environment in which to write became a priority, not just something that I would do someday. Once the commitment was made and there weren't any conflicting goals, everything fell into place. I was able to take some time off and get away from distractions. The perfect cottage was offered for my stay. Typists became available to me. It all came together like magic.

Do you know what you really want from life? Commit yourself to achieving it. Then your mind will find a way to bring it about.

Beware what you set your heart upon.
For it surely shall be yours.
Ralph Waldo Emerson

When Marsha took my class she had just finished a government-sponsored training program and was earning the minimum wage. Six months after completing the class she wrote a letter telling me how the goal-setting methods she had learned really worked.

"I was driving down the street and there, sitting on a used car lot, was my car," she wrote, "a black Thunderbird with red leather interior. I went in and told them that I had been visualizing myself driving that car for six months and that I wanted to try it out.

"The car is mine," she continued. "I got it all by myself, on my signature, without any help from anyone.

"Thank you for teaching me to write my goals down and visualize them each day," she concluded. "It really works."

As I read her letter I thought, "Thank you, Marsha, for not sharing that goal with me until it was acheived. I might have thought it my responsibility as your teacher to inquire if the goal was realistic on your salary." She was teaching me that what appeared unrealistic to me did not have to be unrealistic for someone else. With her goals to shoot for, Marsha didn't stay a minimum wage earner very long.

Eighteen months later I heard from her again. She had taken a course in real estate and moved back to her home city. She wanted me to know that the goal-setting methods were still working. She had quickly become top real-estate agent of the year.

Marsha has been a beautiful mirror for proving that regardless of the circumstances, once we determine what we want and are willing to be responsible for achieving it, the mind goes to work to bring it about.

I have begun several times many things,
and I have often succeeded at last.
Benjamin Disraeli

We were in the process of doing some remodeling. The man we hired to do the painting was a most remarkable person. After his third day on the job I learned that he was seventy-six years old. In no way would I ever have suspected he was a day over sixty. I marveled as I watched him paint a twelve-foot ceiling. I was in awe of his activity and agility. He smiled a mischievous little smile, and his eyes twinkled as he began to tell me how he had cancer seven years before, and all about the treatment he had undergone and the complications that had set in. He left the hospital in a wheelchair. The doctor told him and his wife that he would never walk again, and that he must resign himself to that fact. Still smiling, he said, "You know, I just accepted that as a challenge."

As he related his experience I understood that he had set out to rebuild his health. He didn't tell others, not even his wife, what he was going to do; he just did it. Before me was a living example of the power of determination. As I thought back through my life I realized that whenever I've had an inner determination to accomplish something, I have always succeeded. And when the determination was real, there wasn't any need to talk about it.

Thank you, sir, for the living mirror.

Be a lamp in the chamber
if you cannot be a light in the sky.
George Eliot

Years ago, when I was participating in a Transactional Analysis program, we were instructed to decide what we wanted said about us on our tombstone and to share it with the class the following week.

I kept thinking that it takes most people a good part of their lives to make that decision, and I only had a week. As I thought about it I came to realize that the real question being asked was, "What do you want your life to be about?" Toward the end of the week I knew I wanted to have made some kind of difference when my life was over. So I decided I wanted my tombstone to read simply: "She made a difference."

I didn't have any grandiose ideas about doing anything majestic, or even anything specific. Making a difference simply became an intention, a purpose for my life. Keeping uppermost in my mind the desire to make a difference has opened the door to many very interesting experiences. It has also given me motivation to get out of bed in the morning. When I keep focused on making a difference, that intention affects all I do and the way I do it.

Do you want meaning and purpose in your life? Ask yourself, "What do I want said about me on my tombstone?"

The blossom cannot tell what becomes of its odor,
and no man can tell what becomes of his influence.
Henry Ward Beecher

After I had decided that I wanted my life to be about making a difference, it took me several more years to realize that everyone did make a difference; In fact one could not *not* make a difference. The only choice we have is whether or not we make a positive difference.

The parent who neglects his child is making a difference in the child's life. The employee who does not show up at work when he is expected is making a difference in that business. When one person in a relationship will not communicate, that person is making a difference in the relationship. Yes, what we are and do influences and affects those around us. Knowing this we can consciously decide to make our influence positive.

I discovered that it is only when I am clear on my intention to make a positive difference that it is likely to happen. When I have the clear intent of making a positive difference, I stop and think before I speak, I ask myself if what I am about to say is really helpful.

This same intention in my work has increased my motivation and my effectiveness and given me a feeling of excitement. I find I will redo any work that will get better results if done a different way, and I constantly look for ways to help my students integrate the concepts I teach. Wanting to make a positive difference has been one of the most motivating and energizing factors in my life.

Experiment with the intention to make a positive difference and see how it affects your world?

LOVE -- THE GREAT MOTIVATOR

*Money is like love; it kills slowly and painfully
the one who withholds it,
and it enlivens the other who turns it
upon his fellow man.*
    Kahlil Gibran

Love never hurts, it's the loss of love that hurts.
Love heals both the lover and the loved.

Robert and I were at the table sipping tea and talking. We had been discussing his wife's slow death from cancer and his mother's death shortly afterward. Looking down at the table, he said to himself rather than to me, "I made up my mind that nothing or no one would ever hurt me like that again."

How sad! At that point I knew his heart was closed to being vulnerable to love again.

Unfortunately, Robert is just a one of the many who make this mistake. "I will not ever let anyone or anything hurt me like that again." I have heard that so many times from my clients. The focus is on the loss rather than the joy we experienced. Yes, the loss of a significant love hurts, I know that as well as anyone. Losing my son in an accident was the greatest pain I have experienced. Yet, I was not permanently harmed. We are only permanently harmed when we refuse to be vulnerable to love again.

As a caution, I must say that to be open to love requires that we set boundaries.

Frank was known for his rough and tough approach to dealing with people. One day, I said to him. "You really have a big caring heart, why do you act like that?"

"Because, I have had too many people take advantage of me," he responded.

"Then let's talk about how to set healthy boundaries so people won't take advantage of you."

All of us have to learn to do that or we only set ourselves up to being used and hurt. It is safe to love again when we let go of our demands on others, our unrealistic expectations and develop true healthy boundaries.

Love is the great healer. Loving again after a loss heals our pain. Our need to love is perhaps even greater than our need to be loved. When we extend love, we feel the joy and fulfillment of giving.

To love is to want to give and above all give oneself.
A perfect love is the perfect gift of oneself
without thought of reward or return.
R. H. J. Stewart

Writers have been telling us for centuries that the secret of happiness is to love others. The sacred books tell us over and over again to love one another.

Whenever I heard this idea I acknowledged agreement and decided to become a warm, loving human being. However, being honest with myself, I realized I spent most of my life trying to get other people to love me rather than learning to love them.

Many of us do things we really do not want to do, hoping to win love and approval. Communication is difficult because we frequently withhold the truth, not for fear of hurting others, as we may think, rather, out of fear that we wouldn't be loved. I realized how crazy this was one day when I became aware that I was trying to win the love of someone I didn't even like.

I had spent at least the first half of my life seeking love from others and was not met with fulfillment. I decided I would spend the last half of my life giving love. I decided to experiment with the idea of loving and expecting nothing in return. Right away I began to experience a feeling of joy and fulfillment. I really saw people as I had not seen them before. I became aware of how often I had been indifferent. An estranged relationship was healed without a word being said. I started communicating in an honest and direct way, and people listened. It was wonderful. Even though I'm not as loving as I want to be, I feel as if a song is being sung within me.

Are you willing to experiment with giving love and expecting nothing back? A more loving world can start with you and me.

My biggest discovery was that I had a greater need to love than to be loved. It is in giving love that we experience it.

If you wish to be loved, love.
Seneca

William owns two very large and successful businesses. He sits on several boards, holds offices in his professional organizations, and is a success by all the standards most of the world uses to judge success.

Yet William sat in my office terrified, almost immobilized. The company picnic was coming up and he was afraid to attend. When I questioned him about his fears, he replied, "Well, at work people listen to me and respect me because I am the boss, but they really don't like me or care about me as a person." I asked him whether he cared about his employees as people.

"Oh yes," he responded. He listed all the fringe benefits he made available to his employees. They were really above-average benefits!

"As desirable as those benefits are, William, I wonder how you acknowledge their being. Do you make an effort to find out what is important to them or inquire about their personal interests?"

Shaking his head, he said, "No, I guess I don't."

"William, it sounds to me like you would like your employees to love you. Is that right?"

"You are right, that is exactly what I want," he replied. I assured him that I understood that need and had spent a lot of my energy seeking love too. One day it occurred to me that I could never really experience love from another person. I could only experience the form that that love took. Sometimes the form was recognizable as love and sometimes it wasn't. If I really wanted to experience love I had to give it. My suggestion was that a sure way to experience love at the picnic was to give it.

He looked at me with the most amazed expression and said, "I've been looking under the wrong rock." Which rock are you looking under?

There is only one kind of love,
but it has a thousand guises.
La Rochefoucauld

A saddened woman sat across from me, her pretty face distorted with pain because she did not feel loved. I asked her what it would take for her to feel loved. She replied, "Hugging and touching." I asked her if she was hugged and touched as a child and she replied, "No, not at all. I know my parents loved me, but they were not demonstrative."

The next client to enter my office was a beautiful young woman with a brilliant mind and an enviable career. She was also in pain. She was feeling that she had never been loved and never would be. I asked her what it would take for her to feel loved. She responded, "For someone to keep check on me. To call to see if I made it where I am going, or to see what I am doing, or if I am alright." (I shuddered; the last thing I wanted was someone to keep check on me.) I asked her if that was what her parents had done when she was little. She said, "No, in fact they could have cared less where I was or what I was doing."

Such different concepts fascinated me and I began to ask other people what would make them feel loved. Each person had a different idea of what love was. If others did not fulfill that image, the person didn't feel loved. Most people's picture of love is either what they received as children or what they wanted as children and did not receive. What is your picture?

If you want an interesting insight into your relationships, start asking the people in your life, "What makes you feel loved? What do you need in order to feel love?" You can continue your discovery and see if it was what they got as children—or didn't get as children?

CONNECTING WITH OUR SOURCE

Religion is the first thing and the last thing,
and until man has found God, and been found by God,
He begins at no beginning and works to no end.
H. G. Wells

Everyone who is seriously involved in the pursuit
of science becomes convinced that a Spirit is
manifest in the Laws of the Universe—
a Spirit vastly superior to that of man,
and one in the face of which we,
with our modest powers, must feel humble.
Albert Einstein

While reading the newspaper one day I became conscious of the television being on in the room. There was a science-fiction movie playing. It was about a man from another planet. The man was talking to a young boy who had a speech problem. The man said to the boy, "Ask the light in you to help you." Nothing happened. Again, he repeated, shouting, "Ask the light in you to help you."

I sat there transfixed as the young boy asked the light in him for help and got the help he needed. The scene struck a chord within me. I could imagine God saying, "You need only ask, I'm here."

Conceptually I knew the light was in us, in reality, I still looked for the light everywhere except within myself.

Are you looking for light or for enlightenment? The best source is within you!

All God's giants have been weak men who did
great things because they reckoned on His being there.
J. Hudson Taylor

The idealist, perfectionist side of my personality and the actual me are often worlds apart. For years I kept myself feeling inferior by demanding that I live up to my ideals. I became okay only when I finally accepted the fact that I wasn't okay I had flaws I simply did not meet my standards.

We can have ideals. They motivate us. They give us goals to work toward. In the meantime, be okay with yourself.

I was able to give up my unrealistic expectations by studying the lives of God's giants. Noah, whom God found worthy to spare from the flood, got drunk and lay naked when the flood was over. David, a man after God's own heart, killed a man in order to have the man's wife. Abraham, a man God chose to bless all the nations of the earth lied about Sarah, his wife, to save his own life.

The list could go on. While God did not approve of these acts, He did not reject and abandon these men because of their misdeeds. He continued to accept them, and to love them.

Observing God's continuing fellowship with these flawed men has enabled me to accept God's grace and mercy.

God gives every bird food,
but He does not throw it into the nest.
J. G. Holland

For years I was in conflict over the question of what part God plays in our lives. How much does God do and how much do we do? Sometimes I did nothing while trying to work this out.

After listening to many theories from different sources, I finally decided to look at the master teacher, Jesus, as a role model. As I looked to see what God had done for him, I didn't find any evidence that God had done anything for Jesus. There was much evidence that God did a lot through him.

This Teacher said, "By myself, I can do nothing." Jesus made it clear that, He got this power from God. Finally, the picture began to form for me. God did not do anything for Jesus; Jesus had to go through the process of doing. At the same time, God provided Jesus with the power and motivation. God needed Jesus to fulfill His mission, Jesus needed God to accomplish that mission. An interdependency existed.

When I am working with a person who has had a traumatic experience, I ask in prayer for the client to be given a new perspective, a different interpretation of the situation. I've witnessed some phenomenal experiences with immediate changes.

After I shared with a friend some of the results of these prayers, my friend looked at me and said, "Bobbi, you are the one who does that."

"You could be right," I said. "However, you should have seen the results when I was doing it all by myself." My friend grinned and acknowledged that he, too, had noticed a difference when he did not ask God's help and attempted things alone, and when he did ask God to assist him.

Letting go of me or Him, and becoming me *and* Him, has certainly made a difference in my life. All it takes is a willingness to become an *"us!"*

*You can within your self find a mighty
unexplored kingdom in which
you can dwell in peace if you will.*
Russell H. Conwell

There are many people, I find, who base much of their lives on illusion. One such fantasy that I frequently encounter is the idea that if we were really lovable, people would like us, accept us, and always be there when we need them. When that doesn't happen, we deduce that there must be something wrong with us.

The Teacher, Jesus, who was Love personified, did not win any popularity contests. In fact, His love led to His being killed. Many rejected Him then, and many still do. When He was in the garden going through His own inner struggle and facing death, He asked His disciples to stay awake and keep watch with Him. Instead they went to sleep. They went to sleep because of their human weakness, not because something was amiss in Jesus. He was perfect, yet He did not get His friends to stay awake and give Him moral support. One of His best friends even denied knowing Him.

Much of the time other people are unable to meet our needs because of their own human weaknesses. Recognizing that Jesus was abandoned in His hour of need, has enabled me to give up my self-pity when my loved ones don't meet my needs. Seeing that, despite His perfection, He was not always liked or accepted has released me from the illusion of a requirement for total acceptance. I hope this thought can release you, too.

To be alone with Silence
is to be alone with God.
Samuel Miller Hageman

Magazines, newspapers, and television keep us well informed on the need to reduce stress in our lives. Emphasis is often put on relaxation. Without some form of diversion from our normal activities we may suffer from burnout or disease.

Techniques for reducing stress abound. It is not better techniques that we need. What many people do need is permission in their own minds to do something that isn't "meaningful" or "productive." I, too, am grounded in the Puritan work ethic and I found it hard to learn to relax and do nothing.

It wasn't until I noticed how often Jesus withdrew to be alone that it occurred to me that if He needed time for Himself, you and I aren't likely to be any different. Jesus modeled what modern science is teaching. There was work to be done and Jesus withdrew. People were present to hear His teachings and sick people were there waiting to be healed, yet He withdrew. As long as we are participating in life there will be work to be done. In the meantime, like Jesus, at times we need to be alone.

What works best for me and keeps me running smoothly is one hour of contemplation each morning. This allows me to be in contact with my source, which provides direction and renewal. It is in this quiet time I am able to determine what is important. This hour spent saves far more time throughout the day.

To err is human, to forgive divine.
Alexander Pope

Close your eyes and envision the following scene: You are with a mob of people at Golgotha and are standing near three men hanging on crosses. You and the people are directing most of your attention to the man in the center, His name is Jesus. You are mocking and jeering at Him. You say, "You are the Son of God, save yourself."

Jesus raises his head toward the heavens and says, "Father, forgive them for they know not what they do."

From among the mass of people you shout back, "What do you mean, we don't know what we are doing? We know exactly what we are doing. We are crucifying you. It is you who don't know what you are doing."

Jesus' eyes fall on the people below him. Looking straight at them he says, "No, Father, these people are innocent. They think they know what they are doing, and they do not. Forgive them." Yet, on a physical level the people did know what they were doing. On a much deeper level, they had no clue.

For about two weeks this scene dominated my consciousness. It affected me in a profound way. As I began to look at my life, I remembered times I was sure I knew what I was doing only to find out later that I only had superficial knowledge. I knew that I was responsible for all that I had done. Then I began to wonder, could I be responsible and innocent—that is, not guilty—at the same time? Was forgiveness the experience of seeing or accepting responsibility without affixing blame?

For the first time I could think about a person who had committed a grave injustice against me and forgive him. Even though he thought he knew what he was doing, he had not. He was innocent. And my pain was suddenly gone.

Seeing myself and others as sometimes not really knowing what we are doing, has given me compassion and the ability to forgive. Can it help you, too?

> *The master spirit of the earth shall not*
> *sleep peacefully upon the wind til the*
> *needs of the least of you are satisfied.*
> Kahlil Gibran

As Cherie and I were watching the rain fall, she told me that recently she had been angry with God. She related that she had said to God, "OK, if You are real and loving, why are You so unfair? Why do You give some people so much and other people so little?"

With these questions on her mind, she went for a walk in the rain. As she walked, she noticed a collection of containers that had been put out to catch rainwater. Some had very narrow openings and some had very wide openings. The containers with large openings caught more rainwater. The smaller the opening the less rainwater the container caught.

This made Cherie realize that God was willing to give to all. Some people are *not* open to receive from Him, while others are very open and receive much. Cherie chuckled as she pictured herself as having long narrow neck with a stopper in it. How large is your opening?

I myself believe that the evidence for God
lies primarily in inner personal experiences.
William James

As I was pondering what it could mean to be the child of God, my thoughts turned to what it means to me to be a parent.

When my sons were small and stubbed their toes, I was there to give them comfort. When they soiled their pants, I was there to clean them up. When they had an important lesson to learn, I was willing to let them learn the hard way when necessary. When there was real danger, I was there to protect them. When they were troubled, I was there to listen, even though sometimes they weren't ready to talk. I was there to offer guidance and counsel, although often they didn't seek it.

I don't approve of all they do, and I still love them. In fact there is nothing they can do that would keep me from loving them. There are things they can do that would cause me pain. There is nothing they can do that would cause me to disown them. These are some of the strengths of the love parents have for their children. Yet even my finite mind recognizes that God's love for His children must be far, far greater than this.

Perhaps He sees us as we see our children: Learning, making mistakes. What appear to us as gross and unforgivable may appear to Him as soiled pants.

Perhaps this analogy will help us to get our relationship with God in perspective and to know that He accepts us with all our flaws and mistakes.

*The most important thing in the world
is not to know the Lord's will but to know the Lord.*
Wallace Bays

I've been a religious person most of my life, and I've always attended church on a regular basis and learned a lot about God. Learning about God was interesting, and it did give me some guideposts to live by. Still, there was something missing.

When I set out to discover what it was that was missing, I got a picture of what I was doing. It was like reading everything I could about the president of the United States. I could be with other people who wanted to know about the president. We could all get together and talk about him. No matter how interested we were, or how much we knew about him, something would be missing until we met the president and talked with him personally. We could know a lot about him and still not know him.

Once I had determined that this was the way it must work with God, too, I decided to find out if God could be experienced.

If we want to know a person, we have to let that person know it. We have to be available to him. We have to spend time with him. Also, we have to listen to him. With the desire to know God, I created an inner room in my mind and told God I wanted to meet Him there. Words aren't adequate to explain what happened. All I can say is that I could and do experience an energy that I acknowledge as God. The difference between knowing about and really knowing is like the difference between operating for years on 110 volts, then suddenly discovering you have 220 volts available. My missing part wasn't missing anymore. Quite often, people tell me they feel empty inside, or there is something missing. If that is happening to you, invite God to meet you in the empty place and notice what happens.

Always Remember:
It's YOUR Life!

EPILOGUE

As I finish this book, I see many things more clearly. I am more conscious than ever of how much we all need one another. Many people have touched me personally. I am grateful to each of them for allowing me to experience them and more of myself because of them.

Doing things alone and on my own had been a strong drive in my life. Rereading this book gave me a vivid picture of how very little I've really done alone. That awareness made me feel small and insignificant—a truly humbling experience.

Yet as I saw our connectedness to each other and to the Divine Source, I also felt larger than life, and very powerful. I sensed both my smallness and my bigness simultaneously.

I share these stories with the hope that they can be your mirrors—to reflect your own light. As you read these vignettes, I hope you, too, will allow yourself to be touched and affirmed.

Bibliography

The author has accumulated quotes over many years and regrets that many original sources are unknown. However, she wishes to acknowledge those that are.

Familiar Quotations -- John Bartlett – Little, Brown and Co.
The Treasure Chest – Harper & Row
The Language of Feelings – David Viscott – Pocket Books
Lighten-up Audio – Carol Hansen
Ponderings – Bobbi Sims – Elan Publishing
Workshop – Scott Peck, M.D.
The New Testament--J.B. Phillips Translation

When quotes are not attributed,
they are the work of Bobbi Sims.

Full Color Posters
Suitable for Framing

How People treat you is a statement about them not You!

How you handle it is a statement about you!

Give <u>Nothing</u> or <u>No One</u> the power to spoil it!

Order your 11" by 17" Four Color Posters, Now!

Each poster is a reminder of what you need to remember to empower yourself.

Visit our Website to view the posters in full color.
www.BobbiSims.com

$7 Each or 3 for $17 plus $4 shipping and handling
Check, Visa/MasterCard.

Bobbi Sims
PO Box 6956
Corpus Christi, Tx 78466

Watch for Bobbi Sims' forthcoming book:

Judas's Mother

A story for every mother who feels responsible for the choices of her children

May we add you to our
mailing list for this book?

Mail or e-mail your request to
Bobbi Sims
Po Box 6956
Corpus Christi, Tx 78466

Sims10@aol.com

Dear Reader,
I am conducting ongoing research into the deeper understanding of self-responsibility.

If you have an interesting story surrounding self-
responsibility, please let me hear from you. Please mail or e-
mail your story to the address below.

For Information on Author's
other books, audio cassettes, video programs,
as well as on the author's speeches, seminars, and retreats,
write:

Bobbi Sims
PO Box 6956
Corpus Christi, Texas 78466

Phone: 512-854-0453   Fax: 512-855-8049
1-800-950-7479

E-mail: Sims10@aol.com
Please visit our Web site: www.BobbiSims.com